COUNTRY
KNITS

COUNTRY KNITS

with over 30 glorious designs

DEBBIE BLISS
AND
FIONA McTAGUE

EBURY PRESS · LONDON

First published by Ebury Press
an imprint of Century Hutchinson Ltd
20 Vauxhall Bridge Road
London SW1V 2SA

British Library Cataloguing in Publication Data
Bliss, Debbie
  Country knits.
  1. Clothing. Knitting
  I. Title   II. McTague, Fiona
  646.4
  ISBN 0-85223-865-7

Designer Janet James
Photographer Tony Boase
Stylist Jaki Bell
Hair and make-up Fiona Corrinan

The authors would like to thank the following for their invaluable help: Benise
Goodchild, Gisela Blum, Pauline Cottle, Millie Johnson, Mrs K Murphy, Betty Webb,
Ann McFaull, Mrs Athendon, Rae Fraser, Meg Basden, Stroma Clarke, Kate Upcraft
and David Eyre; Kate Jones for the Zig Zag and Flower Sweater Design. We would
like to especially mention Sue Roberts for pattern checking and Tina Eggleton
for her technical assistance.

The publishers would like to thank the following for their assistance in the production
of the book: Antiquarius; Cable & Co; Charles Jourdan; Ciro Pearls; Cornelia James;
Jim Davidson; Fenn Wright & Manson; Ghost; Joseph; Ken Lane; Levi; Lillywhites;
Margaret Howell; Mondi; Monsoon; Morgan & Oates; Mulberry; Naf, Naf; Next
Directory; Nicole Farhi; Portara; Premonville at Whistles; Risky Business; Top Priority;
Whistles; Wrygges; Wolford.

Filmset in Garamond by Advanced Filmsetters (Glasgow) Ltd
Printed and bound in Italy by New Interlitho S.p.a., Milan

CONTENTS

INTRODUCTION

In *Country Knits* we wanted to take a fresh, contemporary look at traditional handknits, and with this in mind we have put together a collection of designs with a country theme ranging from hard-wearing, sporty Arans to delicate, embroidered cardigans.

We have used classic stitches and patterning in Guernsey sweaters, soft Fair Isles and Norwegian-style jackets, but have combined them with fashion shapes that are simple and generous or neat and fitted. There are tapestry-look and sampler designs inspired by the rich fabrics and rugs of country house interiors; warm wraps and jackets for country weekending. Natural yarns have been used throughout, except where impractical, and the patterns have been sized to include men and children where possible.

We hope *Country Knits* will appeal to all knitters, whether experienced or otherwise, and that you will have as much enjoyment from making the designs as we have had from creating them.

Debbie Bliss

Fiona McTague

BASIC INFORMATION

Abbreviations

Alt—alternate; beg—beginning; cn—cable needle; cm—centimetres; cont—continue; dec—decrease; foll—following; folls—follows; g—gramme; inc—increase; in(s)—inch(es); K—knit; m1—make one by picking up loop lying between sts and work into back of it; meas—measures; mm—millimetres; patt—pattern; P—purl; psso—pass slipped stitch over; rem—remain; rep—repeat; RS—right side; sl—slip; st(s)—stitch(es); st st—stocking stitch; tbl—through back of loop(s); tog—together; WS—wrong side; yb—yarn back; yfwd—yarn forward.

Note: All amounts are based on average requirements and should therefore be regarded as approximate. Use only the yarn specified; we cannot be responsible for an imperfect garment if any other brand is used.

Note: Please check tension carefully, if more sts are made to 10 cm (4 ins) than stated then try again using larger needles, if less sts are made use finer needles.

Note: Figures for larger sizes are given in brackets ( ), where only one set of figures appear, this applies to all sizes. Where the figure 0 appears no sts or rows worked for this size.

Yarns

All yarns used in the patterns are standard weights. If, however, you cannot find the actual yarn specified, you can substitute a yarn of similar weight. If you do substitute a yarn, make sure that the garment is knitted up to the tension specified in the pattern (see below).

Tension/stitch gauge

The flow of yarn which is controlled by the knitter is known as tension/stitch gauge, and is as personal as handwriting. Some knitters put more stress on the yarn, making a smaller stitch and tighter knitted fabric; others put less stress on the yarn and make a looser fabric. For this reason a tension sample is essential for the success of your finished garment.

You must always measure the tension/stitch gauge before you start to make anything. This is necessary for two reasons: to check your tension/stitch gauge against the measurements given in a pattern, and to calculate the number of stitches to cast on and rows to work when you are planning a design of your own. The tension/stitch gauge is always given at the beginning of a pattern and states the number of stitches and rows to the centimetre or inch using the yarn, needles and stitch pattern for a given design.

Calculating the number of stitches and rows is known as tension/stitch gauging. Three factors influence this:
1 The size of needles and type of yarn.
2 The type of stitch pattern.
3 The knitter.

Making a tension/stitch gauge sample

Use the same yarn, needles and stitch pattern as those to be used for the main work. Knit a sample at least 12.5 × 12.5 cm (5 × 5 ins) square. Smooth out the finished sample on a flat surface but do not stretch it.

Measuring the number of stitches

This determines the width of the knitting. Place a steel ruler or tape measure across the sample and mark 10 cm (4 ins) across with pins. Count the number of stitches between the pins. For complete accuracy, pin out the sample several times. An extra half stitch will prove to be vital when you are working from a knitting pattern or when you are gauging the number of stitches to cast on for your own design.

Adjusting tension/stitch gauge

The tension/stitch gauge can be adjusted by changing the size of needles and working another sample. If there are too many stitches to the centimetre or to the inch, your tension/stitch gauge is too tight and you should change to needles a size larger. If there are too few stitches, your tension/stitch gauge is too loose and you should change to needles a size smaller. If the number of stitches is correct but the number of rows incorrect, check the length as you proceed with the pattern.

Measuring the number of rows

This determines the depth of the knitting. The tension/stitch gauge also determines the number of rows to the centimetre or to the inch. Place a ruler vertically along the fabric and mark out 10 cm (4 ins) with pins. Count the number of rows between the pins. From this count you can gauge the number of rows needed to reach the planned length of a design. You can also calculate where shaping is required and the position of increases and decreases.

Altering a pattern

Always make a tension/stitch gauge sample if you intend to alter a pattern for example, changing from stocking/stockinette stitch to a lace stitch, or adding a cable panel. Also check the tension/stitch gauge when changing from a single colour to a multicolour pattern.

COUNTRY
KNITS

SCANDINAVIAN CARDIGAN

MATERIALS

9 × 50 g balls of Hayfield Pure Wool
Classics DK in main colour, M.
2 balls in first contrast colour, A.
1 ball in each of 3 other contrast
colours, B, C and D.
1 pair each of $3\frac{1}{4}$ mm (No. 10/US 3)
and 4 mm (No. 8/US 5) knitting
needles.
7 buttons.

MEASUREMENTS

To fit Bust	86–97 cm	34–38 ins
Actual measurement	107 cm	42 ins
Length to shoulder	57 cm	$22\frac{1}{2}$ ins
Sleeve seam	44 cm	$17\frac{1}{4}$ ins

TENSION

22 sts and 28 rows to 10 cm (4 ins)
over st st using 4 mm (No. 8/US 5)
needles.

ABBREVIATIONS

See page 10.

NOTE

When working patt from Charts for
Back, Left Front and Sleeves read
odd rows (K) from right to left and
even rows (P) from left to right.
Use a separate length of yarn for
each section and twist yarns tog
where they join on every row to
avoid a hole. When working border
patts, strand A and B *loosely* across
WS of work to keep fabric elastic.

CHART 2 BACK AND SLEEVES

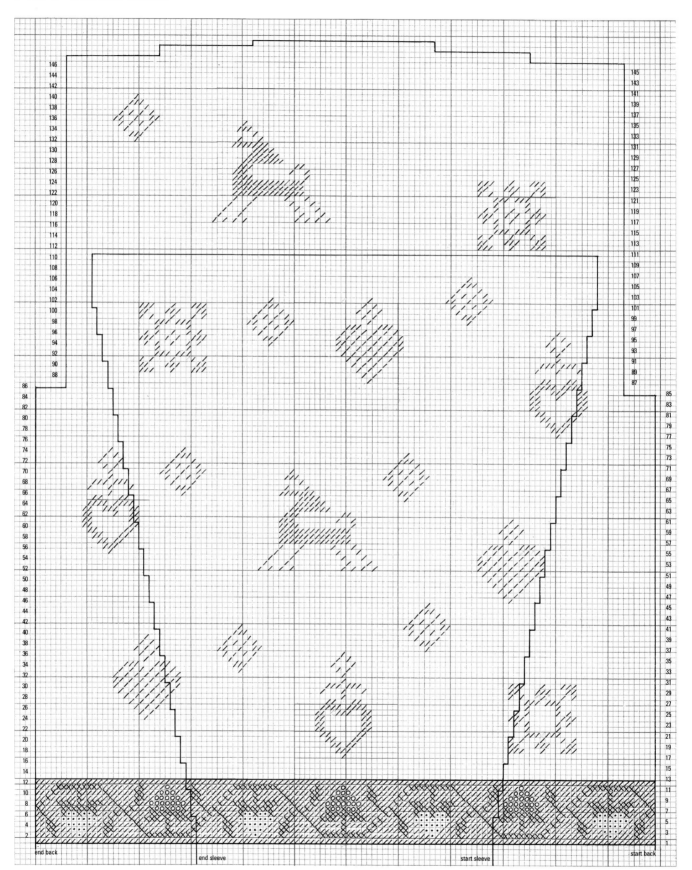

BACK

With 3¼ mm (No. 10/US 3) needles and M, cast on 109 sts.

1st row (RS) P1, [K1, P1] to end.
2nd row K1, [P1, K1] to end.
Rep these 2 rows until work meas 5 cm (2 ins) from beg, ending with a WS row and inc 10 sts evenly across the last row. 119 sts.
Change to 4 mm (No. 8/US 5) needles. Beg with a K row and working in st st throughout, cont in patt from Chart starting and ending rows as indicated until 84 rows in all have been worked in st st.

Shape Armholes

Cast off 6 sts at beg of next 2 rows. 107 sts.
Cont without shaping until 146 rows in all have been worked in st st.

Shape Shoulders

Cast off 18 sts at beg of next 4 rows.
Leave rem 35 sts on a holder for neckband.

LEFT FRONT

With 3¼ mm (No. 10/US 3) needles and M, cast on 51 sts and work 5 cm (2 ins) in rib as for Back welt, ending with a WS row and inc 5 sts evenly across the last row. 56 sts.
Change to 4 mm (No. 8/US 5) needles. Beg with a K row and working in st st throughout, cont in patt from Chart starting and ending rows as indicated until 84 rows in all have been worked in st st.

Shape Armhole

Cast off 6 sts at beg of next row. 50 sts.
Cont without shaping until 121 rows in all have been worked in st st.

KEY

M
A
B
C
D

CHART 1   LEFT FRONT

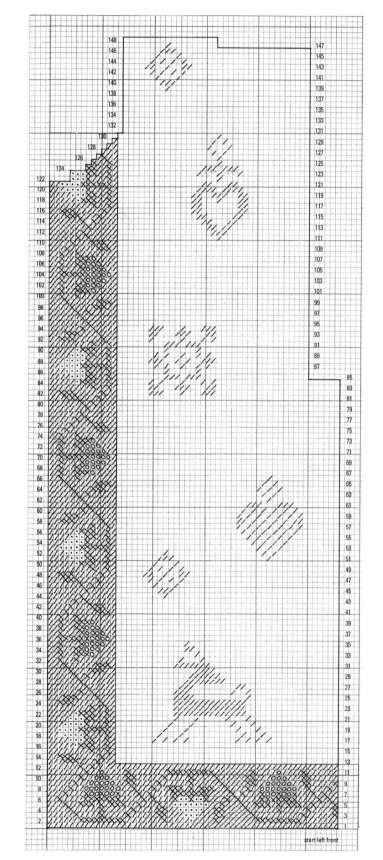

start left front

Shape Neck

Cast off 4 sts at beg of next row, then 3 sts at beg of foll alt row.
Dec one st at neck edge on next 7 rows. 36 sts.
Cont without shaping until 146 rows in all have been worked in st st.

Shape Shoulder

Cast off 18 sts at beg of next row.
Work 1 row straight, then cast off rem 18 sts.

RIGHT FRONT

Work to match Left Front, reversing all shaping and position of patt by reversing Chart, read odd rows (K) from left to right and even rows (P) from right to left.

SLEEVES

With 3¼ mm (No. 10/US 3) needles and M, cast on 45 sts and work 5 cm (2 ins) in rib as for Back welt, ending with a RS row.
Inc row Rib 3, [m1, rib 3, m1, rib 4] 6 times. 57 sts.
Change to 4 mm (No. 8/US 5) needles.
Beg with a K row and working in st st throughout, cont in patt from Chart starting and ending rows as indicated, *at the same time*, inc one st at each end of the 6th and every foll 5th row, working inc sts into patt until there are 97 sts.
Cont without shaping until 110 rows in all have been worked in st st.
Mark each end of last row with a coloured thread.
Using M only, work 8 more rows, then cast off *loosely*.

NECKBAND

Join shoulder seams.
With 3¼ mm (No. 10/US 3) needles, M and RS facing, pick up and K 25 sts evenly up right front neck, K back neck sts from holder, then pick up and K 25 sts evenly down left front neck. 85 sts.
Beg with a 2nd row, work 3 cm (1¼ ins) in rib as for Back welt.
Cast off in rib.

BUTTONHOLE BAND

With 3¼ mm (No. 10/US 3) needles, M and RS facing, pick up and K 131 sts evenly up right front edge to top of neckband.
Work 5 rows in rib as for Back welt.
Next row Rib 4, [cast off 2 sts, rib 18] 6 times, cast off 2 sts, rib 5.
Next row Rib to end, casting on 2 sts over each 2 cast off.
Work 4 more rows, then cast off *loosely* in rib as set.

BUTTON BAND

Work to match Buttonhole Band, omitting buttonholes.

TO MAKE UP

Press work lightly on WS according to instructions on ball band, omitting ribbing.
Sew in sleeves, with rows above markers to cast off sts at underarm.
Join side and sleeve seams.
Press seams. Sew on buttons.

CABLE FITTED SWEATER

MATERIALS

14(14: 15) 50 g balls of Hayfield
Pure Wool Classics DK.
1 pair each of 3¼ mm (No. 10/US 3)
and 4 mm (No. 8/US 5) knitting
needles.
1 cable needle.

MEASUREMENTS

To fit Bust	86 cm	34 ins
	(91: 97)	(36: 38)
Length to shoulder	50 cm	19¾ ins
Sleeve seam	45 cm	17¾ ins

TENSION

22 sts and 28 rows to 10 cm (4 ins)
over st st using 4 mm (No. 8/US 5)
needles.

ABBREVIATIONS

BC–sl next st to cn to back of work,
K1 tbl, then P1 from cn; FC–sl next
st to cn to front of work, P1, then
K1 tbl from cn; C3B–sl next st to cn
to back of work, K2, then P1 from
cn; C3F–sl next 2 sts to cn to front
of work, P1, then K2 from cn;
C4B–sl next 2 sts to cn to back of

work, K2, then K2 from cn; C4F–sl
next 2 sts to cn to front of work,
K2, then K2 from cn; C5–sl next
3 sts to cn to back of work, K2, sl
the 3rd st from cn back onto left-
hand needle and P it, then K2 from
cn; C9–sl next 5 sts to cn to front of
work, K4, sl the P st from cn back
onto left-hand needle and P it, then
K4 from cn; C12B–sl next 8 sts to
cn to back of work, K4, sl the last
4 sts from cn back on to left-hand
needle and K them, then K4 from
cn; C12F–sl next 8 sts to cn to front
of work, K4, sl the last 4 sts from cn
back on to left-hand needle and K
them, then K4 from cn; bind 2–P
next 2 sts tog but do not sl them
from needle, P into first st again,
then sl both sts from needle tog;
T3–sl next 2 sts to cn to front of
work, K1 tbl, sl the last st on cn
back on to left-hand needle and K
this st tbl, then K1 tbl from cn.
Also see page 10.

NOTE

Due to the nature of Panel A the
number of sts vary from row to
row, all sts quoted are the original
number and do not allow for sts
made during the patt.

PANEL A

1st row [P2, K4] 3 times, P1, [K4, P2]
3 times.
2nd row [K2, P4] 3 times, K1, [P4,
K2] 3 times.
3rd row P2, K4, P2, C4F, P2, K4, P1,
K4, P2, C4B, P2, K4, P2.
4th row As 2nd row.
5th and 6th rows As 1st and 2nd
rows.
7th row P2, K4, P2, C4F, P2, C9, P2,
C4B, P2, K4, P2.
8th row As 2nd row.
9th row P2, * m1, [K4, P2] twice, K4,
m1 *, P1, rep from * to *, P2.

10th row * K3, P4, [K2, P4] twice *,
rep from * to *, K3.
11th row * P3, m1, K4, P2 tog *, C4F,
P2 tog, K4, m1, rep from * to *, C4B,
P2 tog, K4, m1, P3.
12th row K4, * [P4, K1] 3 times *, K4,
rep from * to *, K3.
13th row P4, * m1, K3, sl 1, K1, psso,
K4, K2 tog, K3, m1 *, P5, rep from *
to *, P4.
14th row K5, P12, K7, P12, K5.
15th row P5, m1, K4, C4F, K4, m1,
P7, m1, K4, C4B, K4, m1, P5.
16th row K6, P12, K9, P12, K6.

17th row P6, C12B, P9, C12F, P6.
18th row As 16th row.
19th row P4, P2 tog, K4, C4F, K4, P2 tog, P5, P2 tog, K4, C4B, K4, P2 tog, P4.
20th row As 14th row.
21st row P3, * P2 tog, [K4, m1] twice, K4, P2 tog, P3 *, rep from * to *.
22nd row As 12th row.
23rd row P2, P2 tog, K4, m1, P1, C4F, P1, m1, K4, P2 tog, P1, P2 tog, K4, m1, P1, C4B, P1, m1, K4, P2 tog, P2.
24th row As 10th row.
25th row P1, P2 tog, * [K4, P2] twice, K4 *, P3 tog, rep from * to *, P2 tog, P1.
26th row As 2nd row.
27th row As 7th row.
28th row As 2nd row.
These 28 rows form the rep of patt.

PANEL B

1st row K1 tbl, [P1, K1 tbl] twice.
2nd row P1 tbl, [K1, P1 tbl] twice.
3rd and 4th rows As 1st and 2nd rows.
5th row FC, K1 tbl, BC.
6th row K1, [P1 tbl] 3 times, K1.
7th row P1, T3, P1.
8th row As 6th row.
9th row BC, K1 tbl, FC.
10th row As 2nd row.
11th and 12th rows As 1st and 2nd rows.
13th and 14th rows As 1st and 2nd rows.
These 14 rows form the rep of patt.

PANEL C

1st row P7, C5, P7.
2nd row K7, P2, K1, P2, K7.
3rd row P6, C3B, K1, C3F, P6.
4th row K6, P2, K1, P1, K1, P2, K6.
5th row P5, C3B, K1, P1, K1, C3F, P5.
6th row K5, P2, K1, [P1, K1] twice, P2, K5.
7th row P4, C3B, K1, [P1, K1] twice, C3F, P4.
8th row K4, P2, K1, [P1, K1] 3 times, P2, K4.
9th row P3, C3B, K1, [P1, K1] 3 times, C3F, P3.
10th row K3, P2, K1, [P1, K1] 4 times, P2, K3.
11th row P2, C3B, K1, [P1, K1] 4 times, C3F, P2.
12th row K2, P1, [P1, K1] 6 times, P2, K2.

13th row P2, K2, [K1, P1] 5 times, K3, P2.
14th row K2, P2, [P1, K1] 5 times, P3, K2.
These 14 rows form the rep of patt.

BACK

With 3¼ mm (No. 10/US 3) needles cast on 118(122: 130) sts.
1st row (RS) K2, [P2, K2] to end.
2nd row P2, [K2, P2] to end.
Rep these 2 rows until work meas 13 cm (5 ins) from beg, ending with a RS row.
Inc row Rib 3(1: 9), m1, [rib 4, m1] 28(30: 28) times, rib to end. 147(153: 159) sts.
Change to 4 mm (No. 8/US 5) needles and cont in patt as folls:
1st row P 0(3: 0), * P1, [FC, P2, BC] 4(4: 5) times, P1 *, ** work 5 sts as 1st row of Panel B, work 19 sts as 1st row of Panel C, work 5 sts as 1st row of Panel B **, work 37 sts as 1st row of Panel A, rep from ** to ** once, then rep from * to * once, P 0(3: 0).
2nd row K 0(3: 0), * K2, [P1 tbl, K2] 8(8: 10) times *, ** work 5 sts as 2nd row of Panel B, work 19 sts as 2nd row of Panel C, work 5 sts as 2nd row of Panel B **, work 37 sts as 2nd row of Panel A, rep from ** to ** once, then rep from * to * once, K 0(3: 0).
3rd row P 0(3: 0), * P2, [FC, BC, P2] 4(4: 5) times *, ** work 5 sts as 3rd row of Panel B, work 19 sts as 3rd row of Panel C, work 5 sts as 3rd row of Panel B **, work 37 sts as 3rd row of Panel A, rep from ** to ** once, then rep from * to * once, P 0(3: 0).
4th row K 0(3: 0), * K3, [bind 2, K4] 3(3: 4) times, bind 2, K3 *, ** work 5 sts as 4th row of Panel B, work 19 sts as 4th row of Panel C, work 5 sts as 4th row of Panel B **, work 37 sts as 4th row of Panel A, rep from ** to ** once, then rep from * to * once, K 0(3: 0).
5th row P 0(3: 0), * P2, [BC, FC, P2] 4(4: 5) times *, ** work 5 sts as 5th row of Panel B, work 19 sts as 5th row of Panel C, work 5 sts as 5th row of Panel B **, work 37 sts as 5th row of Panel A, rep from ** to ** once, P 0(3: 0).
6th row K 0(3: 0), * K2, [P1 tbl, K2] 8(8: 10) times *, ** work 5 sts as 6th row of Panel B, work 19 sts as 6th row of Panel C, work 5 sts as 6th row of Panel B **, work 37 sts as 6th row of Panel A, rep from ** to ** once, then

rep from * to * once, K 0(3: 0).
7th row P 0(3: 0), * P1, [BC, P2, FC] 4(4: 5) times, P1 *, ** work 5 sts as 7th row of Panel B, work 19 sts as 7th row of Panel C, work 5 sts as 7th row of Panel B **, work 37 sts as 7th row of Panel A, rep from ** to ** once, then rep from * to * once, P 0(3: 0).
8th row K 0(3: 0), * K1, P1 tbl, [K4, bind 2] 3(3: 4) times, K4, P1 tbl, K1 *, ** work 5 sts as 8th row of Panel B, work 19 sts as 8th row of Panel C, work 5 sts as 8th row of Panel B **, work 37 sts as 8th row of Panel A, rep from ** to ** once, then rep from * to * once, K 0(3: 0).
These 8 rows form the rep of Trellis Patt at each end. Keeping Panel sts correct throughout and rem sts as set, cont until work meas 29 cm (11½ ins) from beg, ending with a WS row.

Shape Armholes
Keeping patt correct, cast off 6 sts at beg of next 2 rows.
Dec one st at each end of next 6 rows. 123(129: 135) sts.
Cont without shaping until work meas approximately 50 cm (19¾ ins) from beg, ending with a 10th patt row of Panel A.

Shape Shoulders
Keeping patt correct, cast off 11(12: 13) sts at beg of next 4 rows, then 12(13: 14) sts at beg of next 2 rows.
Leave rem sts on a holder for collar.

FRONT

Work as given for Back until front is 14 rows less than back to beg of shoulder shaping.

Shape Neck
Next row Patt 43(46: 49), P1, P2 tog, K2 and sl these 47(50: 53) sts on to a spare needle for left front, K2, P2 tog, [K2 tog] twice, P2 tog, K4, P2 tog, P1, K4, P2 tog, [K2 tog] twice, P2 tog, K2 and sl these 22 sts on to a holder for collar, K2, P2 tog, P1, patt to end.
Cont on these 47(50: 53) sts for right front.
Dec one st at neck edge on next 13 rows. 34(37: 40) sts.
Work 1 row straight.

Shape Shoulder
Keeping patt correct, cast off 11(12: 13) sts at beg of next and foll alt row.
Work 1 row straight, then cast off rem

12(13: 14) sts.
Return to sts on spare needle; with WS facing rejoin yarn to neck edge and patt to end.
Cont to match first side, reversing all shaping.

SLEEVES

With 3¼ mm (No. 10/US 3) needles cast on 58 sts and work 8 cm (3¼ ins) in rib as for Back welt, ending with a RS row.
Inc row Rib 3, m1, [rib 2, m1] 26 times, rib 3. 85 sts.
Change to 4 mm (No. 8/US 5) needles and cont in patt as folls:
1st row Work 19 sts as 1st row of Panel C, work 5 sts as 1st row of Panel B, work 37 sts as 1st row of Panel A, work 5 sts as 1st row of Panel B, work 19 sts as 1st row of Panel C.
2nd row Work 19 sts as 2nd row of Panel C, work 5 sts as 2nd row of Panel B, work 37 sts as 2nd row of Panel A, work 5 sts as 2nd row of Panel B, work 19 sts as 2nd row of Panel C.
This sets position of patt. Keeping Panel sts correct throughout, *at the same time*, inc one st at each end of the 3rd and every foll 6th row, working inc sts first into Panel B, then into Trellis Patt to match Back until there are 123 sts.
Cont without shaping until work meas 45 cm (17¾ ins) from beg, ending with a WS row.

Shape Top
Keeping patt correct, cast off 6 sts at beg of next 2 rows.
Dec one st at each end of next 10 rows, then every foll alt row until 69 sts rem.
Cast off 2 sts at beg of next 4 rows, then 3 sts at beg of next 10 rows.
Cast off rem sts, working 2 tog over each cable panel.

COLLAR

Join right shoulder seam.
With 3¼ mm (No. 10/US 3) needles and RS facing, pick up and K 21 sts evenly down left front neck, K front neck sts from holder, pick up and K 21 sts evenly up right front neck, then K back neck sts from holder thus: K20, K2 tog, K5, K2 tog, K1, K2 tog, K2, K2 tog, K5, K2 tog, K20. 122 sts.
Beg with a 2nd row, work 12 cm (4¾ ins) in rib as for Back welt. Cast off *loosely* in rib.

TO MAKE UP

Do not press.
Join left shoulder and collar seam, reversing seam on collar to allow for turning. Sew in sleeves, easing fullness at top to fit. Join side and sleeve seams. Fold collar in half to outside. Press seams lightly on WS according to instructions on ball band, omitting ribbing.

FARMYARD SAMPLER CARDIGAN

BACK

With 2¾ mm (No. 12/US 1) needles and M, cast on 121(135) sts.
1st row (RS) K1, [P1, K1] to end.
2nd row P1, [K1, P1] to end.
Rep these 2 rows until work meas 6 cm (2¼ ins) from beg, ending with a WS row and inc 7(9) sts evenly across the last row. 128(144) sts.
Change to 3¼ mm (No. 10/US 3) needles.
Beg with a K row and working in st st throughout, cont in patt from Chart starting and ending rows as indicated until 72(80) rows in all have been worked in st st.

Shape Armholes
Keeping patt correct, cast off 6(8) sts at beg of next 2 rows.
Dec one st at each end of next 1(2) rows, then every foll alt row until 98(112) sts rem.
Cont without shaping until 144(158) rows in all have been worked in st st.

Shape Shoulders
Cast off 29(34) sts at beg of next 2 rows.
Leave rem 40(44) sts on a holder.

LEFT FRONT

With 2¾ mm (No. 12/US 1) needles and M, cast on 55(63) sts and work 6 cm (2¼ ins) in rib as for Back welt, ending with a WS row and inc 4 sts evenly across the last row. 59(67) sts.
Change to 3¼ mm (No. 10/US 3) needles.
Beg with a K row and working in st st throughout, cont in patt from Chart starting and ending rows as indicated until 72(80) rows in all have been worked in st st.

Shape Armhole and Front Edge
Keeping patt correct, cast off 6(8) sts at beg of next row. Work 1 row straight.
Working decs at armhole edge as shown on Chart to match Back, *at the same time*, dec one st at neck edge on

MATERIALS

5(6) 50 g balls of Rowan Soft Cotton/Sea Breeze in main colour, M.
1 ball in each of 5 contrast colours, A, B, C, D and E.
1 pair each of 2¾ mm (No. 12/US 1) and 3¼ mm (No. 10/US 3) knitting needles.
2¾ mm (No. 12/US 1) circular needle, 100 cm (40 ins) long.
9 buttons.

MEASUREMENTS

To fit Bust	81–86 cm	32–34 ins
	(91–97)	(36–38)
Actual measurement	91 cm	36 ins
	(102)	(40)
Length to shoulder	46 cm	18 ins
	(50)	(19¾)
Sleeve seam	42 cm	16½ ins
	(44)	(17¼)

TENSION

28 sts and 36 rows to 10 cm (4 ins) over st st using 3¼ mm (No. 10/US 3) needles.

ABBREVIATIONS

See page 10.

NOTE

When working patt from Chart, read odd rows (K) from right to left and even rows (P) from left to right. Use a separate length of yarn for each section and twist yarns tog where they join on every row to avoid a hole.

next and every foll 4th row until 29(34) sts rem.
Cont without shaping until 144(158) rows in all have been worked in st st.
Cast off.

RIGHT FRONT

Work to match Left Front, reversing position of patt and all shaping as shown on Chart.

SLEEVES

With 2¾ mm (No. 12/US 1) needles and M, cast on 63(67) sts and work 10 cm (4 ins) in rib as for Back welt, ending with a RS row.
Inc row Rib 5(7), m1, [rib 3, m1] 18 times, rib 4(6). 82(86) sts.
Change to 3¼ mm (No. 10/US 3) needles.
Beg with a K row and working in st st throughout, cont in patt from Chart starting and ending rows as indicated, *at the same time*, inc one st at each end of the 11th and every foll 10th row, working inc sts into patt but omitting part "cottages" until there are 100(106) sts.
Cont without shaping, omitting "chair" at each side of Chart until 116(122) rows in all have been worked in st st.

Shape Top
Keeping patt correct and omitting part motifs at each side of Chart, cast off 6(8) sts at beg of next 2 rows.
Dec one st at each end of next and every foll alt row until 76(66) sts rem, then at each end of every row until 24 sts rem.
Cast off.

FRONT BAND

Join shoulder seams.
With 2¾ mm (No. 12/US 1) circular needle, M and RS facing, pick up and K 72(78) sts evenly up right front edge to beg of shaping and 60(68) sts to shoulder, K back neck sts from holder inc one st in centre, then pick up and K 60(68) sts evenly down left front neck to beg of shaping and 72(78) sts to lower edge. 305(337) sts.

BACK, FRONT AND SLEEVES

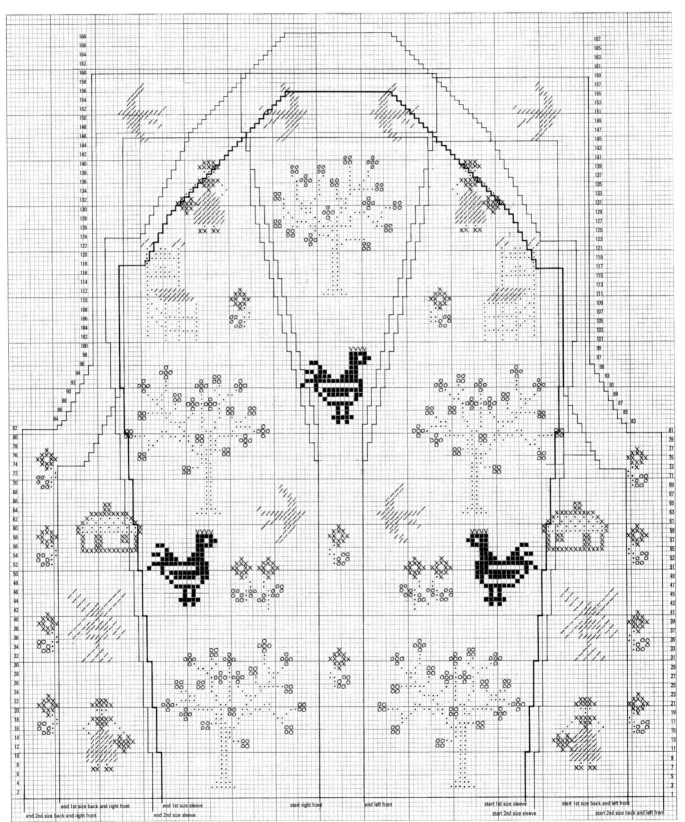

Beg with a 2nd row, work 7 rows in rib as for Back welt.
Next row Rib 3, [yfwd, K2 tog, rib 8] 9 times, rib to end.
(**Note** The top 2(1) buttonholes are a design feature and do not fasten, they could be omitted if preferred.)
Work 6 more rows, then cast off *loosely* in rib as set.

TO MAKE UP

Press work lightly on WS according to instructions on ball band, omitting ribbing.
Using A, embroider "crests" on top of "chicken" heads.
Sew in sleeves. Join side and sleeve seams.
Press seams. Sew on buttons.

KEY

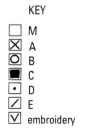

☐ M
☒ A
⊙ B
■ C
· D
╱ E
☑ embroidery

DIAMOND AND CABLE SAMPLER SWEATER

MATERIALS

14 × 50 g balls of Hayfield Pure
Wool Classics DK in main colour,
M.
1 ball OR oddments in each of 8
contrast colours for motifs.
1 pair each of 3¼ mm (No. 10/US 3)
and 4 mm (No. 8/US 5) knitting
needles.
Set of four 3¼ mm (No. 10/US 3)
double-pointed needles.
1 cable needle.

MEASUREMENTS

To fit Bust	86–97 cm	34–38 ins
Actual measurement	107 cm	42 ins
Length to shoulder	62 cm	24½ ins
Sleeve length	44 cm	17¼ ins

TENSION

27 sts and 33 rows to 10 cm (4 ins)
over patt using 4 mm (No. 8/US 5)
needles.

BACK

With 3¼ mm (No. 10/US 3) needles and
M, cast on 114 sts.
1st row (RS) K2, [P2, K2] to end.
2nd row P2, [K2, P2] to end.
Rep these 2 rows until work meas 7 cm
(2¾ ins) from beg, ending with a RS
row.
Inc row Rib 5, m1, rib 4, [m1, rib 3,
m1, rib 4] to end. 145 sts.
Change to 4 mm (No. 8/US 5) needles
and cont in patt as folls:
1st row K13, * C3BP, P3, K5, P3,
C3FP, K17; rep from * to end, *but*
ending last rep with K13.
2nd row P to end.
3rd row K12, * C3BP, P3, C3BK, K1,
C3FK, P3, C3FP, K15; rep from * to
end, *but* ending last rep with K12.
4th row P to end.
5th row K11, * C3BP, P3, C3BK, K3,
C3FK, P3, C3FP, K13; rep from * to
end, *but* ending last rep with K11.

ABBREVIATIONS

C3BP–sl next st to cn to back of
work, K2, then P1 from cn;
C3FP–sl next 2 sts to cn to front of
work, P1, then K2 from cn;
C3BK–sl next st to cn to back of
work, K2, then K1 from cn;
C3FK–sl next 2 sts to cn to front of
work, K1, then K2 from cn;
mb–[K1, P1] 3 times into next st,
turn, P6, turn, [K2 tog] 3 times, sl
2nd and 3rd sts over first st and off
needle. Also see page 10.

NOTE

All motifs can *either* be knitted in
whilst working patt OR Swiss
Darned after knitting is complete.
Use Diagrams 1 and 2 as a guide to
general layout, with Chart Motifs
A–H for actual st and row
positions. Colour ways on Charts
are not strict and flower heads etc.
may be changed or varied as
required.

6th row P to end.
7th row K10, * C3BP, P3, C3BK, K5,
C3FK, P3, C3FP, K11; rep from * to
end, *but* ending last rep with K10.
8th row P to end.
9th row K9, [C3BP, P3, C3BK, K7,
C3FK, P3, C3FP, K9] to end.
10th row P to end.
11th row K8, [C3BP, P3, C3BK, K9,
C3FK, P3, C3FP, K7] to last st, K1.
12th row P to end.
13th row K7, [P3, C3BK, K11,
C3FK, P3, C3FP, K5] to last 2 sts, K2.
14th row P to end.
Special Note: If knitting in motifs
start here; keeping patt correct as folls
beg motifs E and H on next row, then
C and D on row 17, using Diagram 1
and Charts for correct position.
15th row K6, [C3BP, P3, C3BK, K13,
C3FK, P3, C3FP, K3] to last 3 sts, K3.
16th row P to end.
17th row K5, [C3BP, P3, C3BK, K15,
C3FK, P3, C3FP, K1] to last 4 sts, K4.

18th row P to end.
19th row K7, [P3, C3BK, K17, C3FK,
P3, K5] to last 2 sts, K2.
20th row P38, [mb, P33] to last 5 sts,
P5.
21st row K7, [P3, C3FP, K17, C3BP,
P3, K5] to last 2 sts, K2.
22nd row P to end.
23rd row K5, [C3FK, P3, C3FP, K15,
C3BP, P3, C3BK, K1] to last 4 sts, K4.
24th row P to end.
25th row K6, [C3FK, P3, C3FP, K13,
C3BP, P3, C3BK, K3] to last 3 sts, K3.
26th row P to end.
27th row K7, [C3FK, P3, C3FP, K11,
C3BP, P3, C3BK, K5] to last 2 sts, K2.
28th row P to end.
29th row K8, [C3FK, P3, C3FP, K9,
C3BP, P3, C3BK, K7] to last st, K1.
30th row P to end.
31st row K9, [C3FK, P3, C3FP, K7,
C3BP, P3, C3BK, K9] to end.
32nd row P to end.
33rd row K10, * C3FK, P3, C3FP,
K5, C3BP, P3, C3BK, K11; rep from *
to end, *but* ending last rep with K10.
34th row P to end.
35th row K11, * C3FK, P3, C3FP, K3,
C3BP, P3, C3BK, K13; rep from * to
end, *but* ending last rep with K11.
36th row P to end.
37th row K12, * C3FK, P3, C3FP, K1,
C3BP, P3, C3BK, K15; rep from * to
end, *but* ending last rep with K12.
38th row P to end.
39th row K13, * C3FK, P3, K5, P3,
C3BK, K17; rep from * to end, *but*
ending last rep with K13.
40th row P21, * mb, P33; rep from *
to end, *but* ending last rep with P21.
These 40 rows form the rep of patt.
Cont until work meas 41 cm (16½ ins)
from beg, ending with a WS row.

Shape Armholes
Keeping patt correct cast off 4 sts at
beg of next 2 rows. 137 sts.
Cont without shaping until 180 rows
in all have been worked in patt.

Shape Shoulders
Next row Cast off 49 sts, patt 39
including st already on needle after
casting off, cast off 49 sts.
Leave sts on a holder for collar.

MOTIFS

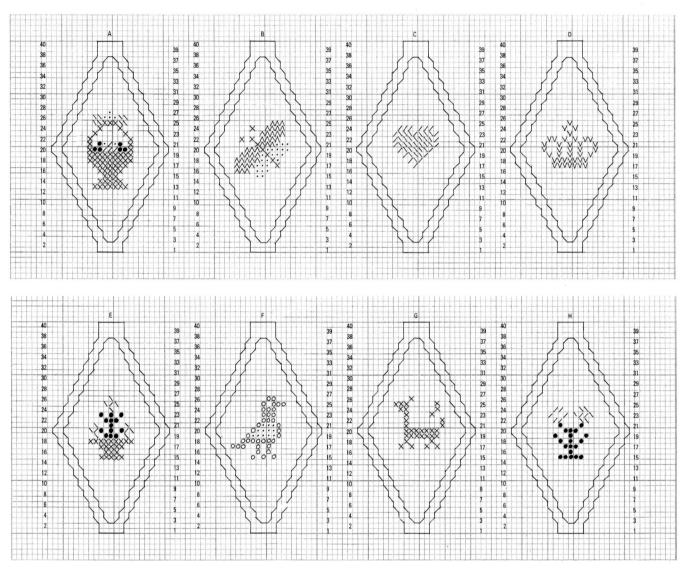

DIAGRAM 1   BACK AND FRONT

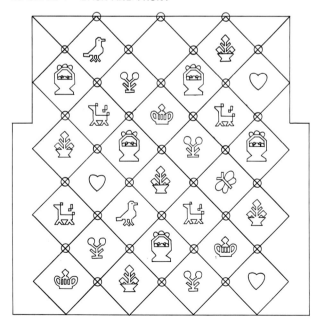

DIAGRAM 2   SLEEVES

KEY

☐	M
⊠	A
⊙	B
⊽	C
⊿	D
⧄	E
⧄	F
·	G
●	H

FRONT

Work as given for Back until 154 rows in all have been worked in patt.

Shape Neck
Next row Patt 58, turn and leave rem sts on a spare needle.
Keeping patt correct, dec one st at neck edge on next 7 rows, then every foll alt row until 49 sts rem.
Cont without shaping until 180 rows in all have been worked in patt.
Cast off.
Return to sts on spare needle; with RS facing sl first 21 sts on to a holder for collar, rejoin M to neck edge and patt to end.
Cont to match first side, reversing shaping.

SLEEVES

With 3¼ mm (No. 10/US 3) needles and M, cast on 54 sts and work 7 cm (2¾ ins) in rib as for Back welt, ending with a RS row.
Inc row Rib 3, [m1, rib 1] to last 2 sts, rib 2. 103 sts.
Change to 4 mm (No. 8/US 5) needles and cont in patt as folls:
1st row K9, * C3BP, P3, K5, P3, C3FP, K17; rep from * to end, *but* ending last rep with K9.
2nd row P to end.
3rd row K8, * C3BP, P3, C3BK, K1, C3FK, P3, C3FP, K15; rep from * to end, *but* ending last rep with K8.
4th row P to end.
This sets position of patt. Cont to match Back, *at the same time*, inc one st at each end of the 15th and every foll 18th row, working inc sts into st st until there are 113 sts.
Cont without shaping until 120 rows in all have been worked in patt.
Cast off *loosely*.

COLLAR

Join shoulder seams.
With set of four 3¼ mm (No. 10/US 3) needles, M and RS facing, sl first 11 sts from holder at front neck on to a spare needle, K rem 10 sts, pick up and K 26 sts evenly up right front neck, K back neck sts from holder inc 5 sts evenly across them, pick up and K 26 sts evenly down left front neck, then K sts from spare needle knitting last 2 sts tog. 116 sts.

Next round P1, K2, [P2, K2] to last st, P1.
Work 6 more rounds in rib as set.
Turn and cont in *rows*:
Next row K5, rib to last 5 sts, K5.
Cont as set, keeping 5 sts at each end of every row in garter st until collar meas 9 cm (3½ ins) from beg, ending with a WS row.
Work 9 rows in garter st.
Cast off *loosely* knitwise.

TO MAKE UP

Do not press.
Sew in sleeves, with last 5 rows to cast off sts at underarm.
If Swiss Darning motifs to sweater do so at this stage.
Join side and sleeve seams. Fold collar to outside.
Press seams lightly on WS according to instructions on ball band, omitting ribbing.

29

TEXTURED SWEATER WITH DEEP RIB COLLAR

MATERIALS

15(16: 17) 50 g balls of Hayfield
Pure Wool Classics DK.
1 pair each of 3¼ mm (No. 10/US 3)
and 4 mm (No. 8/US 5) knitting
needles.
Set of four 3¼ mm (No. 10/US 3)
double-pointed needles.
1 cable needle.

MEASUREMENTS

To fit Bust	86 cm	34 ins
	(91: 97)	(36: 38)
Length to	54 cm	21¼ ins
shoulder	(55: 56)	(21¾: 22)
Sleeve seam	37 cm	14½ ins
	(39: 41)	(15¼: 16¼)

TENSION

22 sts and 28 rows to 10 cm (4 ins)
over st st using 4 mm (No. 8/US 5)
needles.

ABBREVIATIONS

C3B–sl next st to cn to back of
work, K2, then P1 from cn; C3F–sl
next 2 sts to cn to front of work, P1,
then K2 from cn; C4F–sl next 2 sts
to cn to front of work, K2, then K2
from cn; C4B–sl next 2 sts to cn to
back of work, K2, then K2 from
cn; C5–sl next 3 sts to cn to back of
work, K2, sl the 3rd st from cn
back onto left-hand needle and P it,
then K2 from cn. Also see page 10.

PANEL A

1st row P7, [C4F, P2] 3 times, P5.
2nd row K7, [P4, K2] 3 times, K5.
3rd row P6, [C3B, C3F] 3 times, P6.
4th row K6, [P2, K2, P2] 3 times, K6.
5th row P5, C3B, [P2, C4B] twice, P2,
C3F, P5.
6th row K5, P2, K3, P4, K2, P4, K3,
P2, K5.
7th row P4, C3B, P2, [C3B, C3F]
twice, P2, C3F, P4.
8th row K4, P2, K3, P2, K2, P4, K2,
P2, K3, P2, K4.
9th row P3, [C3B, P2] twice, C4F, [P2,
C3F] twice, P3.
10th row [K3, P2] twice, K3, P4, K3,
[P2, K3] twice.
11th row [P2, C3B] 3 times, [C3F, P2]
3 times.
12th row K2, [P2, K3] twice, P2, K2,
[P2, K3] twice, P2, K2.
13th row P2, [K2, P3] twice, K2, P2,
[K2, P3] twice, K2, P2.
14th row As 12th row.
15th row [P2, C3F] 3 times, [C3B, P2]
3 times.
16th row As 10th row.
17th row P3, [C3F, P2] twice, C4F,
[P2, C3B] twice, P3.

18th row As 8th row.
19th row P4, C3F, P2, [C3F, C3B]
twice, P2, C3B, P4.
20th row As 6th row.
21st row P5, C3F, [P2, C4B] twice, P2,
C3B, P5.
22nd row As 4th row.
23rd row P6, [C3F, C3B] 3 times, P6.
24th row As 2nd row.
These 24 rows form the rep of patt.

PANEL B

1st row P2, C3F, P1, C3B, P2.
2nd row K3, P2, K1, P2, K3.
3rd row P3, C5, P3.
4th row As 2nd row.
5th row P2, C3B, P1, C3F, P2.
6th row K2, P2, K3, P2, K2.
7th row P1, C3B, P3, C3F, P1.
8th row K1, P2, K5, P2, K1.
9th row P1, K2, P5, K2, P1.
10th row As 8th row.
11th row P1, C3F, P3, C3B, P1.
12th row K2, P2, K3, P2, K2.
These 12 rows form the rep of patt.

PANEL C

1st row P2, K2, C4B, P2.
2nd row K2, P6, K2.
3rd row P2, C4F, K2, P2.
4th row K2, P6, K2.
These 4 rows form the rep of patt.

BACK

With 3¼ mm (No. 10/US 3) needles cast on 118(126: 130) sts.
1st row (RS) K2, [P2, K2] to end.
2nd row P2, [K2, P2] to end.
Rep these 2 rows until work meas 12 cm (4¾ ins) from beg, ending with a RS row.
Inc row Rib 10(1: 16), m1, [rib 3(4: 3), m1] 33(31: 33) times, rib to end. 152(158: 164) sts.
Change to 4 mm (No. 8/US 5) needles and cont in patt as folls:
1st row K 1(0: 1), [P1, K1] 12(14: 15) times, * K1 tbl, work 11 sts as 1st row of Panel B, K1 tbl, work 10 sts as 1st row of Panel C, K1 tbl, work 11 sts as 1st row of Panel B, K1 tbl *, work 30 sts as 1st row of Panel A; rep from * to * once more, [K1, P1] 12(14: 15) times, K1(0: 1).
2nd row P 1(0: 1), [K1, P1] 12(14: 15) times, * P1, work 11 sts as 2nd row of Panel B, P1, work 10 sts as 2nd row of Panel C, P1, work 11 sts as 2nd row of Panel B, P1 *, work 30 sts as 2nd row of Panel A; rep from * to * once more, [P1, K1] 12(14: 15) times, P 1(0: 1).
3rd row P 1(0: 1), [K1, P1] 12(14: 15) times, * K1 tbl, work 11 sts as 3rd row of Panel B, K1 tbl, work 10 sts as 3rd row of Panel C, K1 tbl, work 11 sts as 3rd row of Panel B, K1 tbl *, work 30 sts as 3rd row of Panel A; rep from * to * once more, [K1, P1] 12(14: 15) times, P 1(0: 1).
4th row K 1(0: 1), [P1, K1] 12(14: 15) times, * P1, work 11 sts as 4th row of Panel B, P1, work 10 sts as 4th row of Panel C, P1, work 11 sts as 4th row of Panel B, P1 *, work 30 sts as 4th row of Panel A; rep from * to * once more, [K1, P1] 12(14: 15) times, K 1(0: 1).
These 4 rows form the rep of Irish Moss st at each side. Keeping Panel sts correct throughout and rem sts in Irish Moss st and twisted st st as set, cont until work meas 33 cm (13 ins) from beg, ending with a WS row.

Shape Armholes
Keeping patt correct, cast off 5 sts at beg of next 2 rows.
Dec one st at each end of next 4 rows, then every foll alt row until 130(134: 138) sts rem.
Cont without shaping until work meas 49(50: 51) cm [19¼(19¾: 20) ins] from beg, ending with a WS row.

Shape Neck
Next row Patt 16(17: 18), turn and leave rem sts on a spare needle.
Keeping patt correct, dec one st at neck edge on next 7 rows, then every foll alt row until 7(8: 9) sts rem.
Cont without shaping until work meas 54(55: 56) cm [21¼(21¾: 22) ins] from beg, ending with a WS row.
Cast off.
Return to sts on spare needle; with RS facing sl first 98(100: 102) sts on to a holder for collar, rejoin yarn to neck edge and patt to end.
Cont to match first side, reversing shaping.

FRONT

Work as given for Back until front meas 38(39: 40) cm [15(15¼: 15¾) ins] from beg, ending with a WS row.

Shape Neck
Next row Patt 26(27: 28), turn and leave rem sts on a spare needle.
Keeping patt correct, dec one st at neck edge on next 2 rows, then every foll alt row until 7(8: 9) sts rem.
Cont without shaping until work meas same as Back to shoulders, ending with a WS row.
Cast off.
Return to sts on spare needle; with RS facing sl first 78(80: 82) sts on to a holder for collar, rejoin yarn to neck edge and patt to end.
Cont to match first side, reversing shaping.

SLEEVES

With 3¼ mm (No. 10/US 3) needles cast on 58(62: 66) sts and work 10 cm (4 ins) in rib as for Back welt, ending with a RS row.
Inc row Rib 3(5: 7), [rib 1, m1, rib 2, m1] 17 times, rib to end. 92(96: 100) sts.
Change to 4 mm (No. 8/US 5) needles and cont in patt as folls:

1st row K1, [P1, K1] 3(4: 5) times, K1 tbl, work 10 sts as 1st row of Panel C, K1 tbl, work 11 sts as 1st row of Panel B, K1 tbl, work 30 sts as 1st row of Panel A, K1 tbl, work 11 sts as 1st row of Panel B, K1 tbl, work 10 sts as 1st row of Panel C, K1 tbl, [K1, P1] 3(4: 5) times, K1.
2nd row P1, [K1, P1] 3(4: 5) times, P1, work 10 sts as 2nd row of Panel C, P1, work 11 sts as 2nd row of Panel B, P1, work 30 sts as 2nd row of Panel A, P1, work 11 sts as 2nd row of Panel B, P1, work 10 sts as 2nd row of Panel C, P1, [P1, K1] 3(4: 5) times, P1.
This sets position of patt. Keeping Panel sts correct throughout and rem sts in Irish Moss st and twisted st st, *at the same time*, inc one st at each end of the 5th and every foll 8th row, working inc sts into Irish Moss st until there are 108(112: 116) sts.
Cont without shaping until work meas 37(39: 41) cm [14½(15¼: 16¼) ins] from beg, ending with a WS row.

Shape Top
Keeping patt correct, cast off 5 sts at beg of next 2 rows.
Dec one st at each end of next and every foll alt row until 62 sts rem.
Cast off 2 sts at beg of next 4 rows, then 3 sts at beg of foll 6 rows.
Cast off rem 36 sts.

COLLAR

Join shoulder seams.
With set of four 3¼ mm (No. 10/US 3) needles and RS facing, pick up and K 50 sts evenly down left front neck, K front neck sts from holder, pick up and K 50 sts evenly up right front neck and 22 sts down right back neck, K back neck sts from holder, then pick up and K 22 sts evenly up left back neck. 320(324: 328) sts.
Work 26 cm (10¼ ins) in rounds of K2, P2 rib.
Cast off *loosely* in rib.

TO MAKE UP

Do not press.
Sew in sleeves, easing fullness at top to fit. Join side and sleeve seams. Fold collar to outside.
Press seams lightly on WS according to instructions on ball band, omitting ribbing.

Zig-zag and Flower Pattern Sweater

BACK

With 3¼ mm (No. 10/US 3) needles and A, cast on 126(138) sts.
1st row (RS) K2, [P2, K2] to end.
2nd row P2, [K2, P2] to end.
Break off A and join in M.
Cont in rib as set until work meas 8 cm (3¼ ins) from beg, ending with a WS row and inc one st in centre of last row. 127(139) sts.
Change to 4 mm (No. 8/US 5) needles.
Beg with a K row, work 2 rows in st st.
Cont in Zig-zag patt as folls:
1st row K3M, [P1C, K5M] 6 times, [P1D, K5M] 5(6) times, [P1E, K5M] 5(6) times, [P1B, K5M] 4 times, P1B, K3M.
2nd row P2M, [K3B, P3M] 5 times, K1B, K2E, [P3M, K3E] 4(5) times, P3M, K1E, K2D, [P3M, K3D] 4(5) times, P3M, K1D, K2C, [P3M, K3C] 5 times, P2M.
3rd row [K1M, P2C] 11 times, [K1M, P2D] 10(12) times, [K1M, P2E] 10(12) times, [K1M, P2B] 11 times, K1M.
4th row [K2B, P3M, K1B] 5 times, K2B, P3M, [K3E, P3M] 5(6) times, [K3D, P3M] 5(6) times, [K3C, P3M] 5 times, K2C.
5th row [P1C, K5M] 6 times, [P1D, K5M] 5(6) times, [P1E, K5M] 5(6) times, [P1B, K5M] 5 times, P1B.
Break off B, C, D, E and cont in M only.
Beg with a P row, cont in st st until work meas 36(37) cm [14¼(14½) ins] from beg, ending with a P row.
* **Next row** K3M, [P1E, K5M] 6 times, [P1B, K5M] 5(6) times, [P1A, K5M] 5(6) times, [P1D, K5M] 4 times, P1D, K3M.
This sets position of Zig-zag patt, work 4 more rows in colours as set.
Next row With M, P to end. *
Rep from * to * once more, *but* using colours A, D, C and E instead of E, B, A and D.
Rep from * to * once more, *but* using colours C, E, B and A instead of E, B, A and D.
Using M only, work 4 rows in st st.
Beg with a K row and working in st st

MATERIALS

11(12) 50 g balls of Hayfield Raw Cotton Classics DK in main colour, M.
2 balls in each of 1st and 2nd contrast colours, A and B.
1 ball in each of 3 other colours, C, D and E.
1 pair each of 3¼ mm (No. 10/US 3) and 4 mm (No. 8/US 5) knitting needles.

MEASUREMENTS

To fit Bust	86–91 cm (97–102)	34–36 ins (38–40)
Actual measure-ment	114 cm (124)	45 ins (49)
Length to shoulder	62 cm (63)	24½ ins (24¾)
Sleeve seam	43 cm (44)	17 ins (17¼)

TENSION

22 sts and 28 rows to 10 cm (4 ins) over st st using 4 mm (No. 8/US 5) needles.

ABBREVIATIONS

See page 10.

NOTE

When working patt from Chart, read odd rows (K) from right to left and even rows (P) from left to right. Use a separate length of yarn for each section and twist yarns tog where they join on every row to avoid a hole. When working Zig-zag patt always keep yarns not in use at WS of work.

throughout as set, cont in patt from Chart starting and ending rows as indicated until the 19 rows are complete.
Using M only, work 5 rows in st st.

Rep from * to * once more.
Break off A, B, D, E and cont in M only.
Working in st st, cont until work meas 62(63) cm [24½(24¾) ins] from beg, ending with a P row.

Shape Shoulders
Cast off 44(49) sts at beg of next 2 rows. Leave rem 39(41) sts on a holder for neckband.

FRONT

Work as given for Back until front meas 55(56) cm [21¾(22) ins] from beg, ending with a P row.

Shape Neck
Next row K 57(62), turn and leave rem sts on a spare needle.
Cast off 3 sts at beg of next row, then 2 sts at beg of foll 2 alt rows.
Dec one st at neck edge on next 4 rows, then every foll alt row until 44(49) sts rem.
Cont without shaping until work meas same as Back to shoulders, ending with a P row.
Cast off.
Return to sts on spare needle; with RS facing sl first 13(15) sts on to a holder for neckband, rejoin M to neck edge and K to end.
Cont to match first side, reversing shaping.

SLEEVES

With 3¼ mm (No. 10/US 3) needles and A, cast on 50 sts and work 5 cm (2 ins) in 2 colour rib as for Back welt, ending with a WS row and inc one st in centre of last row. 51 sts.
Change to 4 mm (No. 8/US 5) needles.
Beg with a K row, work 2 rows in st st.
Cont in Zig-zag patt as folls:
1st row K1M, [P1D, K5M] 4 times, [P1E, K5M] 4 times, P1E, K1M.
This sets position of Zig-zag patt, work 4 more rows in colours as set.
Break of D, E and cont in M only.

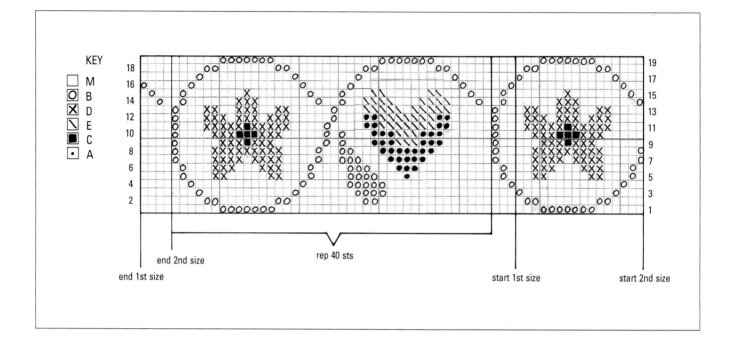

KEY
☐ M
◯ B
☒ D
◩ E
■ C
⊡ A

end 2nd size
end 1st size
rep 40 sts
start 1st size
start 2nd size

Next row P to end.
Beg with a K row cont in st st, inc one
st at each end of next and every foll 3rd
row until there are 113(117) sts.
Cont without shaping until work meas
43(44) cm [17(17¼) ins] from beg,
ending with a P row.
Cast off *loosely*.

NECKBAND

Join right shoulder seam.
With 3¼ mm (No. 10/US 3) needles, M
and RS facing, pick up and K 21 sts
evenly down left front neck, K front
neck sts from holder, pick up and K
21 sts evenly up right front neck, then
K back neck sts from holder.
94(98) sts.
Work 8 rows in K2, P2 rib.
Break off M and join in A.
Work 2 more rows, then cast off *loosely*
in rib as set.

TO MAKE UP

Press work lightly on WS according to
instructions on ball band, omitting
ribbing.
Join left shoulder and neckband seam.
Sew in sleeves, with centre of sleeve to
shoulder seam. Join side and sleeve
seams.
Press seams.

SHORT-SLEEVED COTTON SWEATER

MATERIALS

10(10: 11) 50 g balls of Hayfield
Raw Cotton Classics DK.
1 pair each of 3¼ mm (No. 10/US 3)
and 4 mm (No. 8/US 5) knitting
needles.
1 cable needle.

MEASUREMENTS

To fit Bust	86 cm	34 ins
	(91: 97)	(36: 38)
Length to	50 cm	19¾ ins
shoulder	(51: 52)	(20: 20½)
Sleeve seam	17 cm	6¾ ins

TENSION

22 sts and 28 rows to 10 cm (4 ins)
over st st using 4 mm (No. 8/US 5)
needles.

ABBREVIATIONS

Tw2—with yarn at back of work, sl
1 knitwise, K1, pass slipped st over
knitting into back of it at same
time; C3B—sl next st to cn to back
of work, K2, then P1 from cn;
C3F—sl next 2 sts to cn to front of
work, P1, then K2 from cn; C4—sl
next 2 sts to cn to front of work,
K2, then K2 from cn; C5—sl next
3 sts to cn to back of work, K2, sl
the 3rd st from cn back on to left-
hand needle and P it, then K2 from
cn; C6—sl next 3 sts to cn to front of
work, K3, then K3 from cn;
MB—[K1, P1] 3 times into next st,
turn, K6, turn, [P2 tog] 3 times,
pass the 2nd and 3rd sts over first st
and off needle. Also see page 10.

PANEL A

1st row P 5(6: 7), C5, P 5(6: 7).
2nd row K 5(6: 7), P2, K1, P2, K 5(6: 7).
3rd row P 4(5: 6), C3B, K1, C3F, P 4(5: 6).
4th row K 4(5: 6), P2, K1, P1, K1, P2, K 4(5: 6).
5th row P 3(4: 5), C3B, K1, P1, K1, C3F, P 3(4: 5).
6th row K 3(4: 5), P2, K1, [P1, K1] twice, P2, K 3(4: 5).
7th row P 2(3: 4), C3B, K1, [P1, K1] twice, C3F, P 2(3: 4).
8th row K 2(3: 4), P2, K1, [P1, K1] 3 times, P2, K 2(3: 4).
9th row P 1(2: 3), C3B, K1, [P1, K1] 3 times, C3F, P 1(2: 3).
10th row K 1(2: 3), P2, K1, [P1, K1] 4 times, P2, K 1(2: 3).
11th row P 1(2: 3), K3, [P1, K1] 4 times, K2, P 1(2: 3).
12th row K 1(2: 3), P3, [K1, P1] 4 times, P2, K 1(2: 3).
13th row P 1(2: 3), C3F, K1, [P1, K1] 3 times, C3B, P 1(2: 3).
14th row K 2(3: 4), P3, [K1, P1] 3 times, P2, K 2(3: 4).
15th row P 2(3: 4), C3F, K1, [P1, K1] twice, C3B, P 2(3: 4).
16th row K 3(4: 5), P3, [K1, P1] twice, P2, K 3(4: 5).
17th row P 3(4: 5), C3F, K1, P1, K1, C3B, P 3(4: 5).
18th row K 4(5: 6), P3, K1, P3, K 4(5: 6).
19th row P 4(5: 6), C3F, K1, C3B, P 4(5: 6).
20th row K 5(6: 7), P5, K 5(6: 7).
21st and 22nd rows As 1st and 2nd rows.
23rd row P 4(5: 6), C3B, P1, C3F, P 4(5: 6).
24th row K 4(5: 6), P2, K3, P2, K 4(5: 6).
25th row P 4(5: 6), K2, P1, MB, P1, K2, P 4(5: 6).
26th row As 24th row.
27th row P 4(5: 6), C3F, P1, C3B, P 4(5: 6).
28th row As 2nd row.
These 28 rows form the rep of patt.

PANEL B

1st row P2, K6, P2.
2nd row K2, P6, K2.
3rd row P2, C6, P2.
4th row K2, P6, K2.
5th–8th rows Rep 1st and 2nd rows twice.

9th and 10th rows As 3rd and 4th rows.
11th–20th rows Rep 1st and 2nd rows 5 times.
These 20 rows form the rep of patt.

PANEL C

1st row K4.
2nd row P4.
3rd row C4.
4th row P4.
These 4 rows form the rep of patt.

BACK

With 3¼ mm (No. 10/US 3) needles cast on 106(114: 118) sts.
1st row (RS) K2, [P2, K2] to end.
2nd row P2, [K2, P2] to end.
Rep these 2 rows until work meas 11 cm (4¼ ins) from beg, ending with a RS row.
Inc row Rib 7(13: 13), m1, [rib 2, m1] 46(44: 46) times, rib to end. 153(159: 165) sts.
Change to 4 mm (No. 8/US 5) needles and cont in patt as folls:
1st row P2, [* work 4 sts as 1st row of Panel C, P2, Tw2, work 10 sts as 1st row of Panel B, Tw2, P2, work 4 sts as 1st row of Panel C *, work 15(17: 19) sts as 1st row of Panel A] 3 times, then rep from * to * once more, P2.
2nd row K2, [* work 4 sts as 2nd row of Panel C, K2, P2, work 10 sts as 2nd row of Panel B, P2, K2, work 4 sts as 2nd row of Panel C *, work 15(17: 19) sts as 2nd row of Panel A] 3 times, then rep from * to * once more, K2.
These 2 rows form the rep of Twist st. Keeping Panel sts correct throughout, and rem sts in reverse st st and twist st as set, cont until work meas 29 cm (11½ ins) from beg, ending with a WS row.

Shape Armholes
Keeping patt correct, cast off 8 sts at beg of next 2 rows.
Dec one st at each end of next 10 rows. 117(123: 129) sts.
Cont without shaping until work meas 50(51: 52) cm [19¾(20: 20½) ins] from beg, ending with a WS row.

Shape Shoulders
Cast off 11(12: 13) sts at beg of next 4 rows, then 12 sts at beg of foll 2 rows.
Leave rem 49(51: 53) sts on a holder for neckband.

FRONT

Work as given for Back until front meas 45(46: 47) cm [17¾(18: 18½) ins] from beg, ending with a WS row.

Shape Neck
Next row Patt 48(50: 52), turn and leave rem sts on a spare needle.
Keeping patt correct, cast off 3 sts at beg of next and foll alt row.
Dec one st at neck edge on next 8 rows. 34(36: 38) sts.
Cont without shaping until work meas same as Back to shoulders, ending with a WS row.

Shape Shoulder
Cast off 11(12: 13) sts at beg of next and foll alt row. Work 1 row straight, then cast off rem 12 sts.
Return to sts on spare needle; with RS facing sl first 21(23: 25) sts on to a holder for neckband, rejoin yarn to neck edge, cast off 3 sts and patt to end.
Cont to match first side, reversing all shaping.

SLEEVES

With 3¼ mm (No. 10/US 3) needles cast on 66(66: 70) sts and work 5 cm (2 ins) in rib as for Back welt, ending with a RS row.
Inc row Rib 3(6: 6), m1, [rib 2(1: 1), m1, rib 2, m1] 15(18: 19) times, rib to end. 97(103: 109) sts.
Change to 4 mm (No. 8/US 5) needles and cont in patt as folls:
1st row [Work 15(17: 19) sts as 1st row of Panel A, work 4 sts as 1st row of Panel C, P2, Tw2, work 10 sts as 1st row of Panel B, Tw2, P2, work 4 sts as 1st row of Panel C] twice, work 15(17: 19) sts as 1st row of Panel A.
2nd row [Work 15(17: 19) sts as 2nd row of Panel A, work 4 sts as 2nd row of Panel C, K2, P2, work 10 sts as 2nd row of Panel B, P2, K2, work 4 sts as 2nd row of Panel C] twice, work 15(17: 19) sts as 2nd row of Panel A.
This sets position of patt. Keeping Panel sts correct throughout, *at the same time*, inc one st at each end of the 3rd and every foll 4th row, working inc sts first into Panel C, then into reverse st st to match Back until there are 109(115: 121) sts.
Cont without shaping until work meas 17 cm (6¾ ins) from beg, ending with a WS row.

Shape Top
Keeping patt correct, cast off 8 sts at
beg of next 2 rows.
Dec one st at each end of next and
every foll alt row until 83(87: 91) sts
rem. Work 1 row straight.
Cast off 2 sts at beg of next 14 (15: 16)
rows, then 3 sts at beg of foll 10 rows.
Cast off rem 25(27: 29) sts.

NECKBAND

Join right shoulder seam.
With 3¼ mm (No. 10/US 3) needles and
RS facing, pick up and K 20 sts evenly
down left front neck, K front neck sts
from holder, pick up and K 20 sts
evenly up right front neck, then K
back neck sts from holder. 110(114:
118) sts.
Beg with a 2nd row, work 6 cm (2¼ ins)
in rib as for Back welt.
Cast off *loosely* in rib.

TO MAKE UP

Do not press.
Join left shoulder and neckband seam.
Sew in sleeves, easing fullness at top to
fit. Join side and sleeve seams.
Press seams lightly on WS according
to instructions on ball band, omitting
ribbing.

LACE PATTERN CARDIGAN WITH EMBROIDERED FLOWERS

BACK

With 2¾ mm (No. 12/US 1) needles cast on 121(131) sts.
1st row (RS) K1 tbl, [P1, K1 tbl] to end.
2nd row P1, [K1 tbl, P1] to end.
Rep these 2 rows 19 times more, then the 1st row again.
Inc row Rib 5, m1, [rib 10(11), m1] 11 times, rib 6(5). 133(143) sts.
Change to 3¼ mm (No. 10/US 3) needles and cont in patt as folls:
1st row K1, [K1, yfwd, sl 1, K1, psso, K5, K2 tog, yfwd] to last 2 sts, K2.
2nd row P4, K5, [P5, K5] to last 4 sts, P4.
3rd row K3, [yfwd, sl 1, K1, psso, K3, K2 tog, yfwd, K3] to end.
4th row P5, K3, [P7, K3] to last 5 sts, P5.
5th row K3, [K1, yfwd, sl 1, K1, psso, K1, K2 tog, yfwd, K4] to end.
6th row P6, K1, [P9, K1] to last 6 sts, P6.
7th row K3, [K2, yfwd, sl 1, K2 tog, psso, yfwd, K5] to end.
8th row P to end.
9th row K3, [K1, K2 tog, yfwd, K1, yfwd, sl 1, K1, psso, K4] to end.
10th row K4, P5, [K5, P5] to last 4 sts, K4.
11th row K3, [K2 tog, yfwd, K3, yfwd, sl 1, K1, psso, K3] to end.
12th row K3, [P7, K3] to end.
13th row K1, [K1, K2 tog, yfwd, K5, yfwd, sl 1, K1, psso] to last 2 sts, K2.
14th row P1, K1, [P9, K1] to last st, P1.
15th row K1, K2 tog, yfwd, K7, [yfwd, sl 1, K2 tog, psso, yfwd, K7] to last 3 sts, yfwd, sl 1, K1, psso, K1.
16th row P to end.
These 16 rows form the rep of patt.
Cont until work meas 31(34) cm [12¼(13½) ins] from beg, ending with a WS row.

Shape Armholes

Keeping patt correct cast off 10 sts at beg of next 2 rows. 113(123) sts.
Cont without shaping until work meas 50(54) cm [19¾(21¼) ins] from beg, ending with a WS row.

MATERIALS

10(11) 50 g balls of Rowan Cabled Mercerised Cotton.
1 ball OR oddments of same in each of 2 contrast colours for embroidery.
1 pair each of 2¾ mm (No. 12/US 1) and 3¼ mm (No. 10/US 3) knitting needles.
12 buttons.

MEASUREMENTS

To fit Bust	81–86 cm (91–97)	32–34 ins (36–38)
All round approx.	99 cm (109)	39 ins (43)
Length to shoulder	52 cm (56)	20½ ins (22)
Sleeve seam	47 cm (48)	18½ ins (19)

TENSION

27 sts and 42 rows to 10 cm (4 ins) over patt using 3¼ mm (No. 10/US 3) needles.

ABBREVIATIONS

See page 10.

Shape Neck

Next row Patt 40(44), turn and leave rem sts on a spare needle.
Keeping patt correct, cast off 2 sts at beg of next row.
Dec one st at end of next and every foll alt row until 35(39) sts rem.
Work 1 row straight.

Shape Shoulder

Keeping patt correct, cast off 18(20) sts at beg of next row. Work 1 row straight, then cast off rem 17(19) sts.
Return to sts on spare needle; with RS facing sl first 33(35) sts on a holder for neckband, rejoin yarn to neck edge, cast off 2 sts and patt to end.
Cont to match first side, reversing all shaping.

LEFT FRONT

With 2¾ mm (No. 12/US 1) needles cast on 67(71) sts and work 41 rows in rib as for Back welt.
Inc row Rib 12(17), m1, [rib 9(4), m1] 6(12) times, rib 1(6). 74(84) sts.
Change to 3¼ mm (No. 10/US 3) needles and cont in patt as folls:
1st row K1, [K1, yfwd, sl 1, K1, psso, K5, K2 tog, yfwd] to last 13 sts, K2, turn and leave rem 11 sts on a safety pin. 63(73) sts.
Beg with row 2 cont in patt as for Back, until work meas same as Back to armholes, ending with a WS row.

Shape Armhole

Keeping patt correct, cast off 10 sts at beg of next row. 53(63) sts.
Cont without shaping until work meas 46(50) cm [18(19¾) ins] from beg, ending with a RS row.

Shape Neck

Keeping patt correct, cast off 4(6) sts at beg of next and foll alt row.
Dec one st at end of next and every foll alt row until 35(39) sts rem.
Cont without shaping until work meas same as Back to shoulders, ending with a WS row.

Shape Shoulder

Keeping patt correct, cast off 18(20) sts at beg of next row. Work 1 row straight, then cast off rem 17(19) sts.

RIGHT FRONT

With 2¾ mm (No. 12/US 1) needles cast on 67(71) sts and work 4 rows in rib as for Back welt.
* **Next row** Rib 5, yfwd, K2 tog, rib to end.
Work 17 rows in rib as set. *
Rep from * to * once more.
Next row Rib 5, yfwd, K2 tog, rib to end.
Inc row Rib 1(6), m1, [rib 9(4), m1] 6(12) times, rib 12(17). 74(84) sts.
Cont in patt as folls:
1st row Rib 11 and sl these sts on to a

safety pin, change to 3¼ mm (No. 10/
US 3) needles, K1, [K1, yfwd, sl 1,
K1, psso, K5, K2 tog, yfwd] to last
2 sts, K2. 63(73) sts.
Beg with row 2 of patt as for Back,
cont to match Left Front, reversing all
shaping.

SLEEVES

With 2¾ mm (No. 12/US 1) needles cast
on 59(67) sts and work 10 cm (4 ins) in
rib as for Back welt. ending with a RS
row.
Inc row Rib 4, m1, [rib 4, m1] 13(15)
times, rib 3. 73(83) sts.
Change to 3¼ mm (No. 10/US 3)
needles.
Cont in patt as for Back, *at the same
time*, inc one st at each end of the 7th
and every foll 6th(8th) row, working
inc sts into patt until there are
113(119) sts.
Cont without shaping until work meas
47(48) cm [18½(19) ins] from beg,
ending with a WS row. Place a marker
at each end of last row.
Work a further 16 rows.
Cast off *loosely*.

BUTTON BAND

With 2¾ mm (No. 12/US 1) needles and
RS facing, rib to end across sts on
safety pin at beg of left front, working
twice into first st. 12 sts.
Cont in rib as set until band, when
slightly stretched, reaches up front
edge to neck, ending with a WS row.
Leave sts on a holder.
Tack band in place; with pins mark
position of buttons, 1st to come level
with top buttonhole already worked,
2nd will be in neckband 1.5 cm (⅝ in)
above sts on holder, with 8 more
spaced evenly between these 2.

BUTTONHOLE BAND

With 2¾ mm (No. 12/US 1) needles and
WS facing, rib to end across sts on
safety pin at beg of right front,
working twice into first st. 12 sts.
Cont to match Button Band, making
buttonholes to correspond with
positions of pins as folls:
(RS) Rib 5, yfwd, K2 tog, rib 4.

NECKBAND

Join shoulder seams.
With 2¾ mm (No. 12/US 1) needles and RS facing, rib buttonhole band sts from holder, pick up and K 33(37) sts evenly up right front neck and 6 sts down right back neck, K back neck sts from holder, then pick up and K 6 sts evenly up left back neck and 33(37) sts evenly down left front neck, rib button band sts from holder. 135(145) sts.
Work 5 rows in twisted rib as set.
Next row Rib 5, yfwd, K2 tog, rib to end.
Work 6 more rows, then cast off in rib.

TO MAKE UP

Do not press.
Sew in sleeves, with rows above markers to cast off sts at underarm.
Join side and sleeve seams. Sew on front bands.
Press seams lightly on WS according to instructions on ball band, omitting ribbing.
Embroider flowers to centre of "diamonds" placing them at regular intervals all over cardigan as required:
Flower heads are worked in 1st contrast colour by working 3 Bullion sts, winding yarn 10 times round needle for each st. Work 2 French Knots in centre of each flower head, winding yarn 3 times round needle.
Two leaves are worked under each flower head using 2nd contrast yarn and Lazy Daisy st.
Sew on buttons.

FLORAL AND TARTAN WAISTCOAT

MATERIALS

4(4: 5) 50 g balls of Rowan Cabled Mercerised Cotton in main colour, M.
2 balls in each of 2 contrast colours, A and B.
1 ball in third contrast colour, C.
1 pair each of 2¾ mm (No. 12/US 1) and 3¼ mm (No. 10/US 3) knitting needles.
2¾ mm (No. 12/US 1) circular needle, 80 cm (30 ins) long.
4 buttons.

MEASUREMENTS

To fit bust	86 cm	34 ins
	(91: 97)	(36: 38)
Actual measurement	97 cm	38 ins
	(102: 107)	(40: 42)
Length to shoulder	44 cm	17¼ ins

TENSION

30 sts and 40 rows to 10 cm (4 ins) over st st using 3¼ mm (No. 10/US 3) needles.

ABBREVIATIONS

See page 10.

NOTE

When working patt from Chart 1, read odd rows (K) from right to left and even rows (P) from left to right, strand yarn not in use *loosely* across WS of work to keep fabric elastic. Use a separate length of yarn for each section when working Fronts and twist yarns tog where they join on every row to avoid a hole.

BACK

With 2¾ mm (No. 12/US 1) needles and M, cast on 151(159: 167) sts.
1st row (RS) K1, [P1, K1] to end.
2nd row P1, [K1, P1] to end.
Rep these 2 rows 5 times more inc 10 sts evenly across the last row. 161(169: 177) sts.
Change to 3¼ mm (No. 10/US 3) needles.
Beg with a K row and working in st st throughout, cont in patt from Chart 1 starting and ending rows as indicated until work meas 20 cm (7¾ ins) from beg, ending with a P row.

Shape Armholes

Keeping patt correct, cast off 12(13: 14) sts at beg of next 2 rows.
Dec one st at each end of next and every foll alt row until 119(123: 127) sts rem.
Cont without shaping until work meas 44 cm (17¼ ins) from beg, ending with a P row.

Shape Shoulders

Keeping patt correct, cast off 11 sts at beg of next 4 rows, then 11(12: 13) sts at beg of foll 2 rows.
Leave rem 53(55: 57) sts on a holder.

POCKET LINING

With 3¼ mm (No. 10/US 3) needles and M, cast on 25 sts.
Beg with a K row, work 21 rows in st st.
Leave sts on a holder.

LEFT FRONT

With 3¼ mm (No. 10/US 3) needles and M, cast on 3 sts and K1 row.
[Cast on 3 sts at beg of next row and 6 sts at beg of foll row] 3 times.
8th row Cast on 3 sts, P to end. 33 sts.
9th row Cast on 6 sts, K these 6 sts then * K1M, 1B, 3M, 2B *, 12M; rep from * to * once more, K7M.

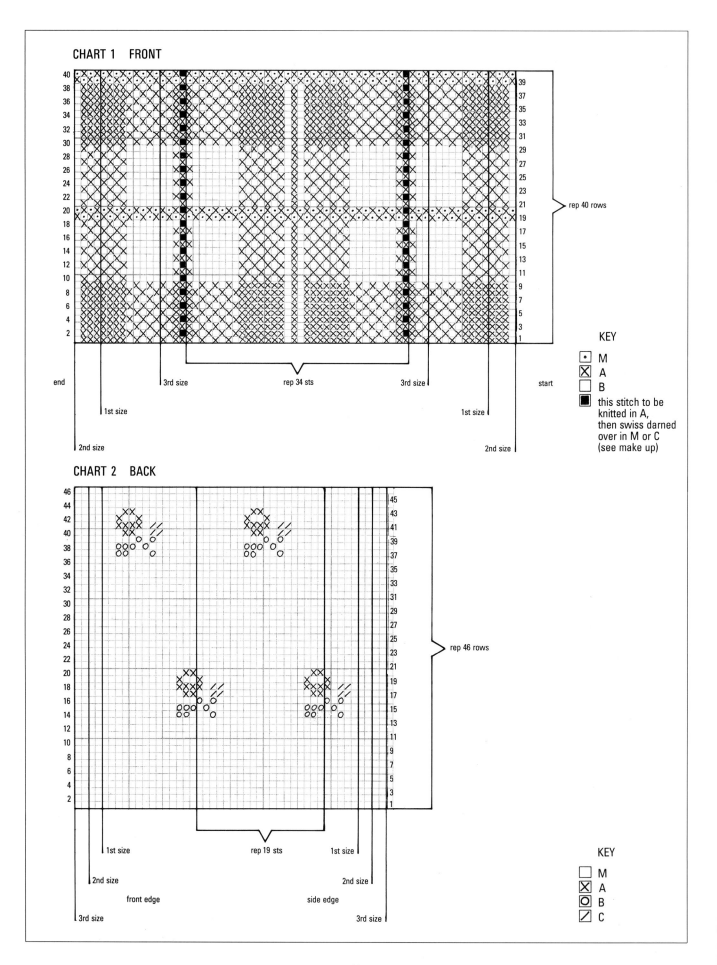

CHART 1   FRONT

rep 40 rows

end
1st size
2nd size
3rd size
rep 34 sts
3rd size
1st size
2nd size
start

KEY
• M
☒ A
☐ B
■ this stitch to be knitted in A, then swiss darned over in M or C (see make up)

CHART 2   BACK

rep 46 rows

1st size
2nd size
3rd size
front edge
rep 19 sts
side edge
1st size
2nd size
3rd size

KEY
☐ M
☒ A
Ⓞ B
⧄ C

10th row Cast on 3 sts, P these 3 sts then * P7M, 3B, 1M, 1B *, 7M; rep from * to * once more, P8M.
11th row Cast on 6 sts, K these 6 sts then * K7M, 1B, 1M, 1B *, 9M; rep from * to * once more, K13M.
12th row Cast on 3 sts, P these 3 sts then * P11M, 2A, 2M, 2C *, 2M; rep from * to * once more, P12M.
13th row Cast on 6 sts, K these 6 sts then [K12M, 2C, 1M, 4A] twice, K13M.
14th row Cast on 3(3: 4) sts, P these 3(3: 4) sts then * P13M, 1A, 2M, 1A *, 2M; rep from * to * once more, P21M.
15th row Cast on 6 sts, K these 6 sts then K22M, [2A, 17M] twice, K 0(0: 1)M.
Working in M only; cast on 3(3: 4) sts at beg of next row, 5(7: 9) sts at beg of foll row; then 2(4: 4) sts at beg of next row. 76(80: 84) sts.
Working throughout in st st as set, cont in patt from Chart 2 starting and ending rows as indicated until work meas 17 cm (6¾ ins) from last set of cast on sts at side edge, ending with a P row.

Shape Armhole and Front Edge
Next row Cast off 12(13: 14) sts, patt to last 2 sts, K2 tog.
Next row Patt to end.
Next row K2 tog, patt to end.
Next row Patt to last 2 sts, P2 tog.
Keeping patt correct, dec one st at armhole edge on next 9 rows, *at the same time*, dec one st at front edge on next and every foll 4th row. 49(52: 55) sts.
Work 1 row straight.
Dec one st at armhole edge on next and foll 4(5: 6) alt rows, *at the same time*, cont to dec at front edge on every 4th row as set until 41(43: 45) sts rem.

Place Pocket
Next row Patt 8(9: 10), sl next 25 sts on to a holder, with WS facing patt across sts of Pocket Lining, patt to end.
Keeping armhole edge straight, cont to dec at front edge only on every 4th row as set until 29(30: 31) sts rem.
Cont without shaping until armhole meas same as on Back, ending with a P row.

Shape Shoulder
Keeping patt correct, cast off 10 sts at beg of next and foll alt row.
Work 1 row straight, then cast off rem 9(10: 11) sts.

RIGHT FRONT

Reading P instead of K and K instead of P, work as given for Left Front, omitting Pocket.

ARMHOLE BORDERS

Join shoulder seams.
With 2¾ mm (No. 12/US 1) needles, M and RS facing, pick up and K 149 sts evenly around armhole edge.
Beg with a 2nd row, work 12 rows in rib as for Back welt.
Cast off in rib.

BUTTONHOLE BAND

With 2¾ mm (No. 12/US 1) circular needle, M and RS facing, pick up and K 48(50: 52) sts evenly along cast on sts of right front from side edge to point, one st from point and mark this st, 27(29: 31) sts to front edge, one st from front corner and mark this st, 60 sts up front edge to beg of shaping, 76 sts to shoulder, then K first 27(28: 29) sts from holder at back neck dec 1(0: 1) st in centre. 239(245: 249) sts.
Beg with a 2nd row, work 5 rows in rib as for Back welt, *at the same time*, inc one st at each side of 2 marked sts on every row. 259(265: 269) sts.
Next row Rib 53(55: 57), m1, K1, m1, rib 37(39: 41), m1, K1, m1, rib 5, [cast off 2 sts, rib 17 including st already on needle after casting off] 4 times, rib to end.
Next row Rib to end, casting on 2 sts over each 2 cast off, still inc at each side of marked sts.
Work 5 more rows in rib as set, still inc as before.
Cast off *loosely* in rib.

BUTTON BAND

With 2¾ mm (No. 12/US 1) circular needle, M and RS facing, K rem 26(27: 28) sts from holder at back neck, inc 0(1: 0) st in centre, pick up and K 76 sts evenly down left front edge to beg of shaping, 60 sts to lower edge, one st from front corner and mark this st, 27(29: 31) sts along cast on sts to point, one st from point and mark this st, then 48(50: 52) sts to side edge. 239(245: 249) sts.
Beg with a 2nd row, work 12 rows in rib as for Back welt, *at the same time*,

inc one st at each side of 2 marked sts on every row.
Cast off *loosely* in rib.

POCKET TOP

With 2¾ mm (No. 12/US 1) needles, M and RS facing, K to end across sts on holder.
Work 7 rows in rib as for Back welt.
Cast off in rib.

TO MAKE UP

Press work lightly on WS according to instructions on ball band, omitting ribbing.
Using M and C, Swiss Darn vertical stripes on Back in position as shown on Chart 1, work stripes alternately in M and C.
Join side seams and ends of armhole borders. Join bands at centre back neck. Sew down pocket top and pocket lining.
Press seams. Sew on buttons.

ARAN JACKET WITH LARGE COLLAR

PANEL A

1st row P1, C5, P1.
2nd row [K1, P2] twice, K1.
3rd row C3B, P1, C3F.
4th row P2, K3, P2.
5th row K2, P1, MB, P1, K2.
6th row As 4th row.
7th row C3F, P1, C3B.
8th row As 2nd row.
These 8 rows form the rep of patt.

PANEL B

1st row K12.
2nd row P12.
3rd and 4th rows As 1st and 2nd rows.
5th row C8B, K4.
6th row As 2nd row.
7th–12th rows Rep 1st and 2nd rows 3 times.
13th row K4, C8F.
14th row As 2nd row.
15th and 16th rows As 1st and 2nd rows.
These 16 rows form the rep of patt.

BACK

With 3¼ mm (No. 10/US 3) needles cast on 138(142: 150) sts.
1st row (RS) K2, [P2, K2] to end.
2nd row P2, [K2, P2] to end.
Rep these 2 rows until work meas 7 cm (2¾ ins) from beg, ending with a WS row and inc 0(2: 0) sts evenly across the last row. 138(144: 150) sts.
Change to 4 mm (No. 8/US 5) needles and cont in patt as folls:
1st row [P4, work 7 sts as 1st row of Panel A, P4, T2L, K1, P 4(5: 6), work 12 sts as 1st row of Panel B, P 4(5: 6), T2L, K1] 3 times, P4, work 7 sts as 1st row of Panel A, P4.
2nd row [K4, work 7 sts as 2nd row of Panel A, K4, T2R, P1, K 4(5: 6), work 12 sts as 2nd row of Panel B, K 4(5: 6), T2R, P1] 3 times, K4, work 7 sts as 2nd row of Panel A, K4.
These 2 rows form the rep of Twist st. Keeping Panel sts correct throughout

MATERIALS

20(22: 24) 50 g balls of Hayfield Pure Wool Classics DK.
1 pair each of 3¼ mm (No. 10/US 3) and 4 mm (No. 8/US 5) knitting needles.
3¼ mm (No. 10/US 3) circular needle, 100 cm OR 42 ins long.
1 cable needle.
2 buttons.

MEASUREMENTS

To fit Bust	86 cm	34 ins
	(91: 97)	(36: 38)
Length to shoulder	48 cm	19 ins
	(50: 52)	(19¾: 20½)
Sleeve with cuff back	47 cm	18½ ins
	(48: 49)	(19: 19¼)

TENSION

22 sts and 28 rows to 10 cm (4 ins) over st st using 4 mm (No. 8/US 5) needles.

ABBREVIATIONS

T2L–K into back of 2nd st on left-hand needle, then K into front of first st allowing both sts to fall from needle; T2R–P into front of 2nd st on left-hand needle, then P into front of first st allowing both sts to fall from needle; C3B–sl next st to cn to back of work, K2, then P1 from cn; C3F–sl next 2 sts to cn to front of work, P1, then K2 from cn; C5–sl next 3 sts to cn to back of work, K2, then P1, K2 from cn; C8F–sl next 4 sts to cn to front of work, K4, then K4 from cn; C8B–sl next 4 sts to cn to back of work, K4, then K4 from cn; MB–[K1, P1, K1] all into next st, [turn, P3, turn, K3] twice, sl 2nd and 3rd sts over first st and off needle. Also see page 10.

and rem sts in reverse st st and Twist st as set, cont until work meas 22(23: 24) cm [8¾(9: 9½) ins] from beg, ending with a WS row.

Shape Armholes
Keeping patt correct, cast off 3(4: 5) sts at beg of next 2 rows.
Dec one st at each end of next and every foll alt row until 118(122: 126) sts rem.
Cont without shaping until work meas 48 (50: 52) cm [19(19¾: 20½) ins] from beg, ending with a WS row.
Cast off.

LEFT FRONT

With 3¼ mm (No. 10/US 3) needles cast on 98(102: 106) sts and work 7 cm (2¾ ins) in rib as for Back welt, ending with a RS row.
Next row Cast off 19 sts, rib to end inc one st in centre. 80(84: 88) sts.
Change to 4 mm (No. 8/US 5) needles and cont in patt as folls:
1st row * P4, work 7 sts as 1st row of Panel A, P4, T2L, K1, P 4(5: 6), work 12 sts as 1st row of Panel B, P 4(5: 6) *, T2L, K1; rep from * to * once more, P1.
2nd row K1, * K 4(5: 6), work 12 sts as 2nd row of Panel B, K 4(5: 6), T2R, P1, K4, work 7 sts as 2nd row of Panel A, K4 *, T2R, P1; rep from * to * once more.
This sets position of patt. Keeping Panel sts correct throughout and rem sts in reverse st st and Twist st, cont until 24 rows in all have been worked in patt.

Shape Front Edge
Keeping patt correct, dec one st at end of next and every foll alt row until work meas same as Back to armholes, ending with a WS row.

Shape Armhole
Next row Cast off 3(4: 5) sts, patt to last 2 sts, K2 tog.
Work 1 row straight.
Keeping patt correct, dec one st at

47

each end of next row and foll 6 alt rows.

Keeping armhole edge straight, cont to dec at front edge only on every alt row until 38(39: 40) sts rem, then every foll 3rd row until 31(32: 33) sts rem. Cont without shaping until work meas same as Back to shoulders, ending with a WS row.

Cast off.

RIGHT FRONT

With 3¼ mm (No. 10/US 3) needles cast on 98(102: 106) sts and work 3 cm (1¼ ins) in rib as for Back welt, ending with a WS row.

Next row Rib 8, cast off 3 sts, rib 36(40: 44) including st already on needle after casting off, cast off 3 sts, rib to end.

Next row Rib to end, casting on 3 sts over each 3 cast off.

Cont in rib as set until work meas 7 cm (2¾ ins) from beg, ending with a WS row and inc one st in centre of last row. 99 (103: 107) sts.

Cont in patt as folls:

1st row Cast off 19 sts, change to 4 mm (No. 8/US 5) needles, P1 (this is st already on needle after casting off), * P4(5: 6), work 12 sts as 1st row of Panel B, P 4(5: 6), T2L, K1, P4, work 7 sts as 1st row of Panel A, P4 *, T2L, K1; rep from * to * once more. 80(84: 88) sts.

2nd row * K4, work 7 sts as 2nd row of Panel A, K4, T2R, P1, K 4(5: 6), work 12 sts as 2nd row of Panel B, K 4(5: 6) *, T2R, P1; rep from * to * once more, K1.

This sets position of patt. Keeping Panel sts correct throughout and rem sts in reverse st st and Twist st, cont to match Left Front, reversing all shaping.

SLEEVES

With 3¼ mm (No. 10/US 3) needles cast on 62(62: 66) sts and work 12 cm (4¾ ins) in rib as for Back welt, ending with a RS row.

Inc row Rib 4(1: 3), [rib 1, m1, rib 2, m1] 18(20: 20) times, rib to end. 98(102: 106) sts.

Change to 4 mm (No. 8/US 5) needles and cont in patt as folls:

1st row P2, [work 12 sts as 1st row of

Panel B, P 4(5: 6), T2L, K1, P4, work 7 sts as 1st row of Panel A, P4, T2L, K1, P 4(5: 6)] twice, work 12 sts as 1st row of Panel B, P2.

2nd row K2, [work 12 sts as 2nd row of Panel B, K 4(5: 6), T2R, P1, K4, work 7 sts as 2nd row of Panel A, K4, T2R, P1, K 4(5: 6)] twice, work 12 sts as 2nd row of Panel B, K2.

This sets position of patt. Keeping Panel sts correct throughout and rem sts in reverse st st and Twist st, *at the same time*, inc one st at each end of the 3rd and every foll 4th row, working

inc sts into patt sequence to match Back until there are 138(142: 146) sts. Cont without shaping until work meas 53(54: 55) cm [20¾(21¼: 21¾) ins] from beg, ending with a WS row.

Shape Top

Keeping patt correct, cast off 3(4: 5) sts at beg of next 2 rows.

Dec one st at each end of next and every foll alt row until 118(120: 122) sts rem.

Cast off 4 sts at beg of next 8 rows. Cast off rem 86(88: 90) sts.

RIGHT SIDE COLLAR

With 4 mm (No. 8/US 5) needles cast on 4 sts.
1st row (RS) P4.
2nd row K4.
3rd row Cast on 3 sts, P1, K2, P4.
4th row K4, P2, K1.
5th row Cast on 3 sts, K2, P1, K2, P5.
6th row K5, P2, K1, P2.
7th row Cast on 3 sts, P2, work 7 sts as 1st row of Panel A, P4.
8th row K4, work 7 sts as 2nd row of Panel A, K2.
9th row Cast on 3 sts, K1, P4, work 7 sts as 3rd row of Panel A, P4.
10th row K4, work 7 sts as 4th row of Panel A, K4, P1. 16 sts.
This sets position of patt. Place a marker at end of last row.
Keeping Panel sts correct throughout, rem sts as set and working all inc sts into patt sequence to match Back, inc one st at beg of next row and end of foll row. Work 1 row straight. Inc one st at end of next row and beg of foll row. Work 1 row straight.
Rep the last 6 rows until there are 62(70: 78) sts. Work 1 row straight.
Inc one st at end of next and every foll alt row until there are 82(86: 90) sts. Work 14(16: 18) rows straight.
Leave sts on a holder.

LEFT SIDE COLLAR

With 4 mm (No. 8/US 5) needles cast on 4 sts.
1st row (RS) P4.
2nd row Cast on 3 sts, K1, P2, K4.
3rd row P4, K2, P1.
4th row Cast on 3 sts, P1, K3, P2, K4.
5th row P5, K2, P1, K2.
6th row Cast on 3 sts, K3, P2, K1, P2, K5.
7th row P4, work 7 sts as 1st row of Panel A, P2.
8th row Cast on 3 sts, P1, K4, work 7 sts as 2nd row of Panel A, K4.
9th row P4, work 7 sts as 3rd row of Panel A, P4, K1.
10th row P1, K4, work 7 sts as 4th row of Panel A, K4. 16 sts.
This sets position of patt. Place a marker at beg of last row.
Keeping Panel sts correct throughout, rem sts as set and working all inc sts into patt sequence to match Back, inc one st at end of next row and beg of foll row. Work 1 row straight. Inc one

st at beg of next row and end of foll row. Work 1 row straight.
Rep the last 6 rows until there are 62(70: 78) sts. Work 1 row straight.
Inc one st at beg of next and every foll alt row until there are 82(86: 90) sts. Work 14(16: 18) rows straight.

Join Pieces

Next row Patt to end, cast on 56(58: 60) sts, then with RS facing patt to end across Right Side Collar sts on holder. 220(230: 240) sts.
Work 51(55: 59) rows straight.
Keeping patt correct, dec one st at each end of next and every foll alt row until 198(208: 218) sts rem. Work 1 row straight.
Cast off 2 sts at beg of next 4 rows, 3 sts at beg of foll 6 rows, then 4 sts at beg of next 8 rows.
Leave rem 140(150: 160) sts on a spare needle.

COLLAR EDGING

With 3¼ mm (No. 10/US 3) circular needle and RS facing, pick up and K 118(124: 132) sts evenly up outside edge of Left Side and 48 sts around shaped edge, K sts from spare needle dec 30(32: 34) sts evenly across them, then pick up and K 48 sts evenly around shaped edge and 118(124: 132) sts down outside edge of Right Side. 442(462: 486) sts.
Beg with a 2nd row, work 5 rows in rib as for Back welt.
Cast off *loosely* in rib.

TO MAKE UP

Do not press.
Join shoulder seams. Sew in sleeves, easing fullness at top to fit.
Join side and sleeve seams, reversing seam on cuff to allow for turning. Sew shaped edges of collar to front edges of jacket, with rows below markers and edging to cast off sts at top of welt and cast on sts to back neck.
Press seams lightly on WS according to instructions on ball band, omitting ribbing. Sew on buttons.

CROPPED FAIR ISLE
SWEATER

MATERIALS

6(7: 7) 50 g balls of Rowan Cabled
Mercerised Cotton in main colour,
M.
3 balls in first contrast colour, A.
3 balls in 2nd contrast colour, B.
2 balls in 3rd contrast colour, C.
1 ball in 4th contrast colour, D.
1 ball in 5th contrast colour, E.
1 pair each of $2\frac{3}{4}$ mm (No. 12/US 1)
and $3\frac{1}{4}$ mm (No. 10/US 3) knitting
needles.
Set of four $2\frac{3}{4}$ mm (No. 12/US 1)
double-pointed needles.

MEASUREMENTS

To fit Bust	86 cm	34 ins
	(91: 97)	(36: 38)
All round	104 cm	41 ins
approx.	(109: 114)	(43: 45)
Length to	47 cm	$18\frac{1}{2}$ ins
shoulder	(49: 51)	($19\frac{1}{4}$: 20)
Sleeve seam	48 cm	19 ins
	(49: 50)	($19\frac{1}{4}$: $19\frac{3}{4}$)

TENSION

34 sts and 34 rows to 10 cm (4 ins)
over patt using $3\frac{1}{4}$ mm (No. 10/
US 3) needles.

ABBREVIATIONS

See page 10.

NOTE

When working patt from Chart,
read odd rows (K) from right to left
and even rows (P) from left to
right. Strand yarn not in use *loosely*
across WS of work to keep fabric
elastic.

BACK

With $2\frac{3}{4}$ mm (No. 12/US 1) needles and
M, cast on 131(137: 143) sts.
1st row (RS) K1, [P1, K1] to end.
2nd row P1, [K1, P1] to end.
Rep these 2 rows until work meas
10 cm (4 ins) from beg, ending with a
RS row.
Inc row Rib 6(7: 8), [m1, rib 3, m1, rib
2] 24(25: 26) times, rib 5. 179(187:
195) sts.
Change to $3\frac{1}{4}$ mm (No. 10/US 3)
needles.
Beg with a K row and working in st st
throughout, cont in patt from Chart
starting and ending rows as indicated
until work meas 22(23: 24) cm [$8\frac{3}{4}$(9:
$9\frac{1}{2}$) ins] from beg, ending with a P row.

Shape Armholes
Keeping patt correct, cast off 6 sts at
beg of next 2 rows.
Dec one st at each end of next and
every foll alt row until 155(161:
167) sts rem.
Cont without shaping until work meas
47(49: 51) cm [$18\frac{1}{2}$($19\frac{1}{4}$: 20) ins] from
beg, ending with a P row.

Shape Shoulders
Keeping patt correct, cast off 26(27:
28) sts at beg of next 2 rows, then
25(26: 27) sts at beg of foll 2 rows.
Leave rem 53(55: 57) sts on a holder
for collar.

FRONT

Work as given for Back until front
meas 40(42: 44) cm [$15\frac{3}{4}$($16\frac{1}{2}$: $17\frac{1}{4}$) ins]
from beg, ending with a P row.

Shape Neck
Next row Patt 65(67: 69), turn and
leave rem sts on a spare needle.
Keeping patt correct, dec one st at
neck edge on next 10 rows, then every
foll alt row until 51(53: 55) sts rem.
Cont without shaping until work meas
same as Back to shoulders, ending
with a P row.

Shape Shoulder

Keeping patt correct, cast off 26(27: 28) sts at beg of next row. Work 1 row straight, then cast off rem 25(26: 27) sts.

Return to sts on spare needle; with RS facing sl first 25(27: 29) sts on to a holder for collar, rejoin yarns to neck edge and patt to end.

Cont to match first side, reversing all shaping.

SLEEVES

With 2¾ mm (No. 12/US 1) needles and M, cast on 67(69: 71) sts and work 10 cm (4 ins) in rib as for Back welt, ending with a RS row.

Inc row Rib 3(6: 4), [m1, rib 4(3: 3), m1, rib 3] 9(10: 11) times, rib 1(3: 1). 85(89: 93) sts.

Change to 3¼ mm (No. 10/US 3) needles.

Beg with a K row and working in st st throughout, cont in patt from Chart starting and ending rows as indicated, *at the same time*, inc one st at each end of the 5th and every foll 3rd row until there are 167(171: 175) sts.

Cont without shaping until work meas 48(49: 50) cm [19(19¼: 19¾) ins] from beg, ending with a P row.

Shape Top

Keeping patt correct, cast off 6 sts at beg of next 2 rows.

Dec one st at each end of next and every foll alt row until 143(145: 147) sts rem. Work 1 row straight.

Cast off *loosely*.

COLLAR

Join shoulder seams.

With set of four 2¾ mm (No. 12/US 1) needles, M and RS facing, pick up and K 29 sts evenly down left front neck, K front neck sts from holder, pick up and K 29 sts evenly up right front neck, then K back neck sts from holder. 136(140: 144) sts.

Work 2 cm (¾ in) in rounds of K1, P1 rib, ending at centre front neck.

Turn and cont in *rows* of rib as set until collar meas 10 cm (4 ins) from beg. Cast off *loosely* in rib.

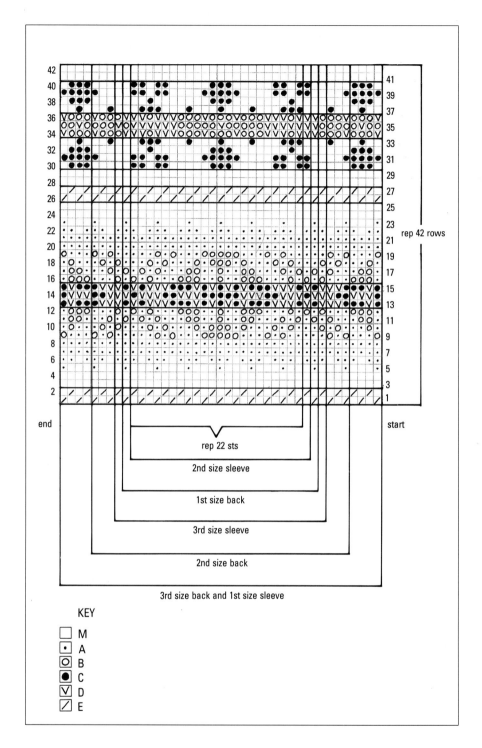

KEY

☐ M
· A
○ B
● C
∨ D
╱ E

TO MAKE UP

Press work lightly on WS according to instructions on ball band, omitting ribbing.

Sew in sleeves. Join side and sleeve seams. Press seams.

LONG LINE FAIR ISLE
CARDIGAN

MATERIALS

7(7: 8) 50 g balls of Rowan Cabled
Mercerised Cotton in main colour,
M.
2(3: 3) balls in first contrast colour,
A.
2(3: 3) balls in 2nd contrast colour,
B.
2 balls in 3rd contrast colour, C.
2 balls in 4th contrast colour, D.
1 ball in 5th contrast colour, E.
1 ball in 6th contrast colour, F.
1 pair each of $2\frac{3}{4}$ mm (No. 12/US 1)
and $3\frac{1}{4}$ mm (No. 10/US 3) knitting
needles.
12 buttons.

MEASUREMENTS

To fit Bust	86 cm	34 ins
	(91: 97)	(36: 38)
All round approx.	102 cm	40 ins
	(107: 112)	(42: 44)
Length to shoulder	68 cm	$26\frac{3}{4}$ ins
	(70: 72)	($27\frac{1}{2}$: $28\frac{1}{4}$)
Sleeve seam	46 cm	18 ins
	(47: 48)	($18\frac{1}{2}$: 19)

TENSION

32 sts and 34 rows to 10 cm (4 ins)
over patt using $3\frac{1}{4}$ mm (No. 10/
US 3) needles.

ABBREVIATIONS

See page 10.

NOTE

When working patt from Chart,
read odd rows (K) from right to left
and even rows (P) from left to
right. Strand yarn not in use *loosely*
across WS of work to keep fabric
elastic.

BACK

With 2¾ mm (No. 12/US 1) needles and M, cast on 147(155: 163) sts.
1st row (RS) P1, [K1, P1] to end.
2nd row K1, [P1, K1] to end.
Rep these 2 rows until work meas 6 cm (2¼ ins) from beg, ending with a RS row.
Inc row Rib 6(1: 5), m1, [rib 8(9: 9), m1] 17 times, rib to end. 165(173: 181) sts.
Change to 3¼ mm (No. 10/US 3) needles.
Beg with a K row and working in st st throughout, cont in patt from Chart starting and ending rows as indicated until work meas 47(48: 49) cm [18½(19: 19¼) ins] from beg, ending with a P row.

Shape Armholes

Keeping patt correct, cast off 6 sts at beg of next 2 rows.
Dec one st at each end of next and every foll alt row until 141(149: 157) sts rem.
Cont without shaping until work meas 68(70: 72) cm [26¾(27½: 28¼) ins] from beg, ending with a P row.

Shape Shoulders

Keeping patt correct, cast off 22(23: 25) sts at beg of next 2 rows, then 22(24: 25) sts at beg of foll 2 rows.
Leave rem 53(55: 57) sts on a holder for neckband.

POCKET LININGS (make 2)

With 3¼ mm (No. 10/US 3) needles and M, cast on 32 sts.
Beg with a K row, cont in st st until work meas 13 cm (5 ins) from beg, ending with a P row.
Leave sts on a holder.

LEFT FRONT

With 2¾ mm (No. 12/US 1) needles and M, cast on 71(75: 79) sts and work 6 cm (2¼ ins) in rib as for Back welt, ending with a RS row.
Inc row Rib 4(3: 5), m1, [rib 9(10: 10), m1] 7 times, rib to end. 79(83: 87) sts.
Change to 3¼ mm (No. 10/US 3) needles.
Beg with a K row and working in st st throughout, cont in patt from Chart starting and ending rows as indicated until 48 rows in all have been worked in st st.

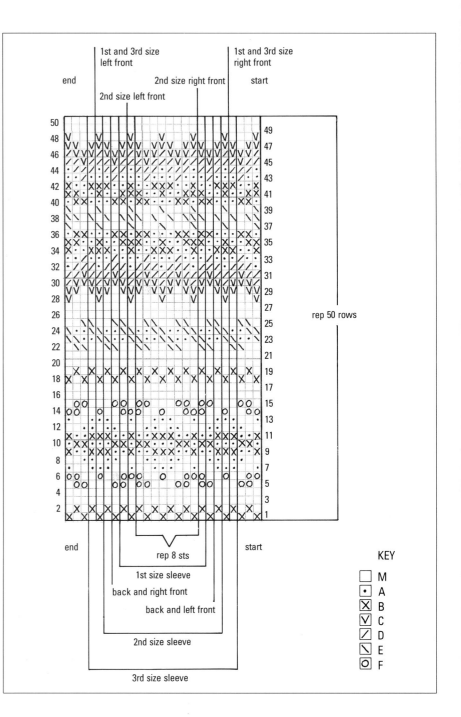

Place Pocket
Next row Patt 21(23: 25), sl next 32 sts on to a holder, with RS facing patt across sts of first pocket lining, patt to end.
Cont until work meas same as Back to armholes, ending with a P row.

Shape Armhole

Keeping patt correct cast off 6 sts at beg of next row. Work 1 row straight.
Dec one st at beg of next and every foll alt row until 67(71: 75) sts rem.
Cont without shaping until work meas 61(63: 65) cm [24(24¾: 25½) ins] from beg, ending with a K row.

Shape Neck

Keeping patt correct, cast off 10 sts at beg of next row, then 4 sts at beg of foll 2 alt rows.
Dec one st at neck edge on next 3(4: 5) rows, then every foll alt row until 44(47: 50) sts rem.
Cont without shaping until work meas same as Back to shoulders, ending with a P row.

Shape Shoulder

Keeping patt correct, cast off 22(23: 25) sts at beg of next row. Work 1 row straight, then cast off rem 22(24: 25) sts.

RIGHT FRONT

Work to match Left Front, reversing all shaping, position of Pocket and patt.

SLEEVES

With 2¾ mm (No. 12/US 1) needles and M, cast on 67(69: 71) sts and work 8 cm (3¼ ins) in rib as for Back welt, ending with a RS row.
Inc row Rib 7(4: 1), [m1, rib 2, m1, rib 3] 12(13: 14) times. 91(95: 99) sts.
Change to 3¼ mm (No. 10/US 3) needles.
Beg with a K row and working in st st throughout, cont in patt from Chart starting and ending rows as indicated, *at the same time*, inc one st at each end of the 5th and every foll 5th row, working inc sts into patt until there are 133(139: 145) sts.
Cont without shaping until work meas 46(47: 48) cm [18(18½: 19) ins] from beg, ending with a P row.

Shape Top
Keeping patt correct cast off 6 sts at beg of next 2 rows.
Dec one st at each end of next and every foll alt row until 109(115: 121) sts rem. Work 1 row straight.
Cast off *loosely*.

BUTTONHOLE BAND

With 2¾ mm (No. 12/US 1) needles, M and RS facing, pick up and K 183(189: 195) sts evenly up right front edge.
Work 3 rows in rib as for Back welt.
Next row Rib 4, [cast off 2 sts, rib 15(15: 16)] 10 times, cast off 2 sts, rib 7(13: 9).
Next row Rib to end, casting on 2 sts over each 2 cast off.
Work 4 more rows, then cast off *loosely* in rib as set.

BUTTON BAND

Work to match Buttonhole Band, omitting buttonholes.

NECKBAND

Join shoulder seams.
With 2¾ mm (No. 12/US 1) needles, M and RS facing, pick up and K 38(39: 40) sts evenly up right front neck including band, K back neck sts from holder, then pick up and K 38(39: 40) sts evenly down left front neck including band. 129(133: 137) sts.
Work 3 rows in rib as for Back welt.
Next row Rib 3, cast off 2 sts, rib to end.
Next row Rib to end, casting on 2 sts over the 2 cast off.
Work 4 more rows, then cast off in rib as set.

POCKET TOPS

With 2¾ mm (No. 12/US 1) needles, M and RS facing, K to end across sts on holder inc one st in centre. 33 sts.
Beg with a 2nd row, work 9 rows in rib as for Back welt.
Cast off *loosely* in rib.

TO MAKE UP

Press work lightly on WS according to instructions on ball band, omitting ribbing.
Sew in sleeves. Join side and sleeve seams. Sew down pocket tops and pocket linings.
Press seams. Sew on buttons.

CHILD'S FAIR ISLE CARDIGAN

MATERIALS

3(3: 3: 4) 50 g balls of Rowan Cabled Mercerised Cotton in main colour, M.
1 ball in each of 6 contrast colours, A, B, C, D, E and F.
1 pair each of 2¾ mm (No. 12/US 1) and 3¼ mm (No. 10/US 3) knitting needles.
7 buttons.

MEASUREMENTS

To fit Chest	56 cm (61: 66: 71)	22 ins (24: 26: 28)
All round approx.	61 cm (66: 71: 76)	24 ins (26: 28: 30)
Length to shoulder	30 cm (33: 35: 37)	11¾ ins (13: 13¾: 14½)
Sleeve seam	23 cm (25: 27: 30)	9 ins (9¾: 10¾: 11¾)

TENSION

32 sts and 34 rows to 10 cm (4 ins) over patt using 3¼ mm (No. 10/US 3) needles.

ABBREVIATIONS

See page 10.

NOTE

When working patt from Chart, read odd rows (K) from right to left and even rows (P) from left to right. Strand yarn not in use *loosely* across WS of work to keep fabric elastic.

BACK

With 2¾ mm (No. 12/US 1) needles and M, cast on 79(87: 95: 103) sts.
1st row (RS) P1, [K1, P1] to end.
2nd row K1, [P1, K1] to end.
Rep these 2 rows until work meas 4 cm (1½ ins) from beg, ending with a RS row.
Inc row Rib 2(6: 10: 4), m1, [rib 4(4: 4: 5), m1] 19 times, rib to end. 99(107: 115: 123) sts.
Change to 3¼ mm (No. 10/US 3) needles.
Beg with a K row and working in st st throughout, cont in patt from Chart starting and ending rows as indicated until work meas 16(18: 19: 20) cm [6¼(7: 7½: 7¾) ins] from beg, ending with a P row.

Shape Armholes
Keeping patt correct cast off 4 sts at beg of next 2 rows.
Dec one st at each end of next and every foll alt row until 83(91: 99: 107) sts rem.
Cont without shaping until work meas 30(33: 35: 37) cm [11¾(13: 13¾: 14½) ins] from beg, ending with a P row.

Shape Shoulders
Keeping patt correct, cast off 11(13: 14: 16) sts at beg of next 2 rows, then 12(13: 15: 16) sts at beg of foll 2 rows.
Leave rem 37(39: 41: 43) sts on a holder for neckband.

POCKET LININGS (make 2)

With 3¼ mm (No. 10/US 3) needles and M, cast on 22 sts.
Beg with a K row, cont in st st until work meas 6 cm (2¼ ins) from beg, ending with a P row.
Leave sts on a holder.

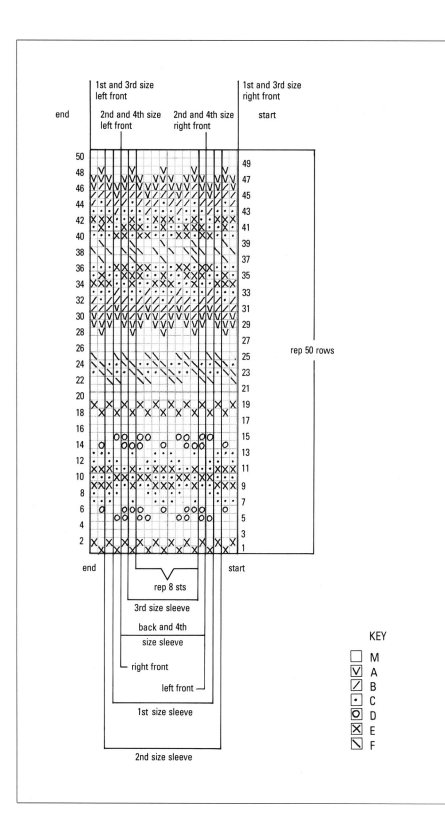

end

1st and 3rd size
left front

2nd and 4th size
left front

2nd and 4th size
right front

1st and 3rd size
right front

start

rep 50 rows

end

start

rep 8 sts

3rd size sleeve

back and 4th

size sleeve

right front

left front

1st size sleeve

2nd size sleeve

KEY

☐	M
V	A
╱	B
·	C
Ⓞ	D
☒	E
◢	F

LEFT FRONT

With 2¾ mm (No. 12/US 1) needles and M, cast on 37(41: 45: 49) sts and work 4 cm (1½ ins) in rib as for Back welt, ending with a RS row.
Inc row Rib 5(3: 5: 2), m1, [rib 3(4: 4: 5), m1] 9 times, rib to end. 47(51: 55: 59) sts.
Change to 3¼ mm (No. 10/US 3) needles.
Beg with a K row and working in st st throughout, cont in patt from Chart starting and ending rows as indicated until 22 rows in all have been worked in st st.

Place Pocket
Next row Patt 11(13: 15: 17), sl next 22 sts on to a holder, with RS facing patt across sts of first pocket lining, patt to end.
Cont until work meas same as Back to armholes, ending with a P row.

Shape Armhole
Keeping patt correct cast off 4 sts at beg of next row. Work 1 row straight.
Dec one st at beg of next and every foll alt row until 39(43: 47: 51) sts rem.
Cont without shaping until work meas 25(28: 29: 31) cm [9¾(11: 11½: 12¼) ins] from beg, ending with a K row.

Shape Neck
Keeping patt correct, cast off 5 sts at beg of next row, then 2 sts at beg of foll 2 alt rows.
Dec one st at neck edge on next 5(6: 7: 8) rows, then every foll alt row until 23(26: 29: 32) sts rem.
Cont without shaping until work meas same as Back to shoulders, ending with a P row.

Shape Shoulder
Keeping patt correct cast off 11(13: 14: 16) sts at beg of next row. Work 1 row straight, then cast off rem 12(13: 15: 16) sts.

RIGHT FRONT

Work to match Left Front, reversing all shaping, position of Pocket and patt.

SLEEVES

With 2¾ mm (No. 12/US 1) needles and M, cast on 49(51: 53: 55) sts and work 6 cm (2¼ ins) in rib as for Back welt, ending with a RS row.

Inc row Rib 3(4: 5: 6), m1, [rib 4, m1] 11 times, rib to end. 61(63: 65: 67) sts. Change to 3¼ mm (No. 10/US 3) needles.

Beg with a K row and working in st st throughout, cont in patt from Chart starting and ending rows as indicated, *at the same time*, inc one st at each end of the 3rd and every foll 3rd row, working inc sts into patt until there are 91(97: 103: 109) sts.

Cont without shaping until work meas 23(25: 27: 30) cm [9(9¾: 10¾: 11¾) ins] from beg, ending with a P row.

Shape Top

Keeping patt correct cast off 4 sts at beg of next 2 rows.

Dec one st at each end of next and every foll alt row until 75(81: 87: 93) sts rem. Work 1 row straight. Cast off *loosely*.

BUTTONHOLE BAND

With 2¾ mm (No. 12/US 1) needles, M and RS facing, pick up and K 83 (93: 95: 103) sts evenly up right front edge. Work 3 rows in rib as for Back welt.

Next row Rib 3, [cast off 2 sts, rib 12(14: 14: 16)] 5 times, cast off 2 sts, rib 8(8: 10: 8).

Next row Rib to end, casting on 2 sts over each 2 cast off.

Work 3 more rows, then cast off *loosely* in rib as set.

BUTTON BAND

Work to match Buttonhole Band, omitting buttonholes.

NECKBAND

Join shoulder seams.

With 2¾ mm (No. 12/US 1) needles, M and RS facing, pick up and K 30(30: 33: 33) sts evenly up right front neck including band, K back neck sts from holder, then pick up and K 30(30: 33: 33) sts evenly down left front neck including band. 97(99: 107: 109) sts. Work 3 rows in rib as for Back welt.

Next row Rib 3, cast off 2 sts, rib to end.

Next row Rib to end, casting on 2 sts over the 2 cast off.

Work 3 more rows, then cast off in rib as set.

POCKET TOPS

With 2¾ mm (No. 12/US 1) needles, M and RS facing, K to end across sts on holder inc one st in centre. 23 sts. Beg with a 2nd row, work 7 rows in rib as for Back welt. Cast off *loosely* in rib.

TO MAKE UP

Press work lightly on WS according to instructions on ball band, omitting ribbing.

Sew in sleeves. Join side and sleeve seams. Sew down pocket tops and pocket linings.

Press seams. Sew on buttons.

CLASSIC FAIR ISLE SOCKS

MATERIALS

1(2) 50 g balls of Rowan Cabled Mercerised Cotton in main colour, M.
1 ball in each of 3(5) contrast colours (see Chart).
1 pair each of 2¾ mm (No. 12/US 1) and 3¼ mm (No. 10/US 3) knitting needles.
Set of four 3¼ mm (No. 10/US 3) double-pointed needles.

MEASUREMENTS

To fit foot	15 cm	6 ins
	(24)	(9½)
Leg to base of heel	14 cm	5½ ins
	(18)	(7)

TENSION

30 sts and 40 rows to 10 cm (4 ins) over st st using 3¼ mm (No. 10/US 3) needles.

ABBREVIATIONS

See page 10.

NOTE

When working patt from Charts, read odd rows (K) from right to left and even rows (P) from left to right. Strand yarn not in use *loosely* across WS of work to keep fabric elastic.

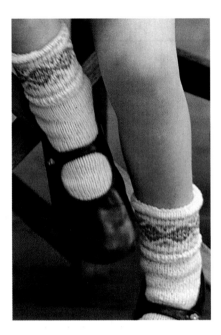

Beg with Cuff

With 2¾ mm (No. 12/US 1) needles and M, cast on 49(65) sts.
1st row (RS) K1, [P1, K1] to end.
2nd row P1, [K1, P1] to end.
Rep these 2 rows 1(2) times more.
Change to 3¼ mm (No. 10/US 3) needles.
Beg with a K row and working in st st throughout, cont in patt from Chart 1(2) until the 19(25) rows are complete. Work 3(5) rows in M only.
Next row P to end dec 6 sts evenly across the row. 43(59) sts.
Beg with a K row, reversing st st to allow for turn over cuff, cont until work meas 18(22) cm [7(8¾) ins] from beg, ending with a P row.

Divide for Heel

With set of four 3¼ mm (No. 10/US 3) needles cont as folls:
K 9(13), turn, sl the last 10(14) sts of row on to the other end of this same needle; divide rem 24(32) sts on to 2 needles and leave for instep.
Next row P 8(12), P2 tog, P 9(13). 18(26) sts.
Work 10(14) rows straight.

Turn Heel

1st row K 13(19), K2 tog tbl, turn.
2nd row Sl 1, P 8(12), P2 tog, turn.
3rd row Sl 1, K 8(12), K2 tog tbl, turn.
Cont in this way working one more st on every row until all sts are worked. 10(14) sts.
Next row K 5(7).
This completes heel.
Sl the instep sts back on to one needle; with the spare needle K 5(7), pick up and K 8(11) sts evenly up side of heel, with 2nd needle K instep sts, with 3rd needle pick up and K 8(11) sts down side of heel, then K 5(7).
Next round K to end.
Next round On first needle K to last 2 sts, K2 tog, K instep sts, on 3rd needle K2 tog tbl, K to end.
Rep these 2 rounds until 40(52) sts rem.
Cont without shaping until work meas 12(20) cm [4¾(7¾) ins] from base of heel.

Shape Toe

Divide sts as folls: sl 2(3) sts from beg of 2nd needle on to first needle and 2(3) sts from end of 2nd needle on to 3rd needle.

Next round On first needle K to last 3 sts, K2 tog, K1, on 2nd needle, K1, K2 tog tbl, K to last 3 sts, K2 tog, K1, on 3rd needle K1, K2 tog tbl, K to end.
Next round K to end.
Rep these 2 rounds until 20(28) sts rem.
K the sts from first needle on to 3rd needle and graft sts.

TO MAKE UP

Press work lightly on WS according to instructions on ball band, omitting ribbing.
Join seam, reversing seam on cuff to allow for turning. Press seam.

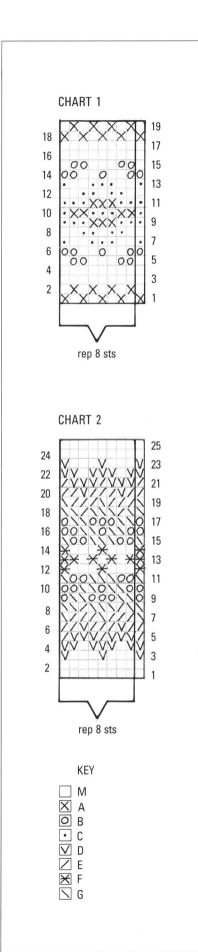

CHART 1

rep 8 sts

CHART 2

rep 8 sts

KEY

☐	M
☒	A
⊙	B
·	C
∨	D
╱	E
✹	F
╲	G

CROSS AND DIAMOND 'KELIM' SWEATER

BACK

With 3¼ mm (No. 10/US 3) needles and M, cast on 130 sts.
1st row (RS) K2, [P2, K2] to end.
2nd row P2, [K2, P2] to end.
Rep these 2 rows until work meas 5 cm (2 ins) from beg, ending with a WS row and inc st in centre of last row. 131 sts.
Change to 4 mm (No. 8/US 5) needles.
Beg with a K row and working in st st throughout, cont in patt from Chart (see page 64) starting and ending rows as indicated until 82 rows in all have been worked in st st.

Shape Armholes

Keeping patt correct, cast off 10 sts at beg of next 2 rows. 111 sts.
Cont without shaping until 162 rows in all have been worked in st st.

Shape Shoulders

Cast off 18 sts at beg of next 4 rows.
Leave rem 39 sts on a holder for neckband.

FRONT

Work as given for Back until 142 rows in all have been worked in st st.

Shape Neck

Next row Patt 45, turn and leave rem sts on a spare needle.
Dec one st at neck edge on next 9 rows. 36 sts.
Cont without shaping until 162 rows in all have been worked in st st.

Shape Shoulder

Cast off 18 sts at beg of next row.
Work 1 row straight, then cast off rem 18 sts.
Return to sts on spare needle; with RS facing sl first 21 sts on to a holder for neckband, rejoin M to neck edge and patt to end.
Cont to match first side, reversing all shaping.

MATERIALS

10 × 50 g balls of Hayfield Grampian DK in main colour, M.
2 balls in each of 3 contrast colours, A, B and C.
1 pair each of 3¼ mm (No. 10/US 3) and 4 mm (No. 8/US 5) knitting needles.
Set of four 3¼ mm (No. 10/US 3) double-pointed needles.

MEASUREMENTS

To fit up to Bust/ Chest	102 cm	40 ins
Actual measure-ment	119 cm	47 ins
Length to shoulder	62 cm	24½ ins
Sleeve seam	43 cm	17 ins

TENSION

22 sts and 28 rows to 10 cm (4 ins) over st st using 4 mm (No. 8/US 5) needles.

ABBREVIATIONS

See page 10.

NOTE

When working in *rows* and patt from Chart, read odd rows (K) from right to left and even rows (P) from left to right. Use a separate length of yarn for each section and twist yarns tog where they join on every row to avoid a hole. When working rows 3–20 from Chart, strand yarn not in use *loosely* across WS of work to keep fabric elastic.

SLEEVES

With 3¼ mm (No. 10/US 3) needles and M, cast on 46 sts and work 5 cm (2 ins) in rib as for Back welt, ending with a RS row.

Inc row Rib 2, m1, [rib 3, m1] 14 times, rib 2. 61 sts.
Change to 4 mm (No. 8/US 5) needles.
Beg with a K row and working in st st throughout, cont in patt from Chart starting and ending rows as indicated, *at the same time*, inc one st at each end of the 3rd and every foll 3rd row, working inc sts into patt until there are 117 sts, then every foll alt row until there are 127 sts.
Cont without shaping until work meas 43 cm (17 ins) from beg, ending with a P row. Mark each end of last row with a coloured thread.
Work 12 more rows, then cast off *loosely*.

NECKBAND

Join shoulder seams.
With set of four 3¼ mm (No. 10/US 3) needles, M and RS facing, pick up and K 20 sts evenly down left front neck, K front neck sts from holder, pick up and K 20 sts evenly up right front neck, then K back neck sts from holder inc 4 sts evenly across them. 104 sts.
P 1 round.
Working throughout in rounds of st st (every round K) cont in patt from Chart, starting where indicated, work 16 rounds.
Using M only, work a further 3 cm (1¼ ins).
Cast off *loosely* using a 4 mm (No. 8/ US 5) needle.

TO MAKE UP

Press work lightly on WS according to instructions on ball band, omitting ribbing.
Sew in sleeves, with rows above markers to cast off sts at underarm.
Join side and sleeve seams.
Press seams.

KEY □ M ☒ A ⊡ B ⊡ C

TEXTURED SUIT

MATERIALS

JACKET: 21(22: 22) 50 g balls of
Hayfield Pure Wool Classics DK.
SKIRT: 10(10: 11) balls.
1 pair each of 3¼ mm (No. 10/US 3),
3¾ mm (No. 9/US 4) and 4 mm
(No. 8/US 5) knitting needles.
1 cable needle.
8 buttons for Jacket.
Waist length of elastic for Skirt.

MEASUREMENTS

To fit Bust	86 cm	34 ins
	(91: 97)	(36: 38)
JACKET:		
Length to	73 cm	28¾ ins
shoulder		
Sleeve seam	48 cm	19 ins
SKIRT:		
Length	56 cm	22 ins

TENSION

36 sts and 30 rows to 10 cm (4 ins)
over patt using 4 mm (No. 8/US 5)
needles.

ABBREVIATIONS

T2L–sl next st to cn to front of
work, P1, then K1 from cn; T2R–sl
next st to cn to back of work, K1,
then P1 from cn; C8–sl next 4 sts to
cn to front of work, K4, then K4
from cn. Also see page 10.

JACKET

BACK

With 3¼ mm (No. 10/US 3) needles cast on 123(129: 135) sts.
1st row (RS) K2, [P1, K1] to last st, K1.
2nd row K1, [P1, K1] to end.
Rep these 2 rows until work meas 6 cm (2¼ ins) from beg, ending with a RS row.
Inc row Rib 1(4: 7), m1, [rib 2, m1, rib 3, m1] 24 times, rib to end. 172(178: 184) sts.
Change to 4 mm (No. 8/US 5) needles and cont in patt as folls:
1st row P 2(5: 8), [K9, P7] to last 10(13: 16) sts, K8, P to end.
2nd row K 2(5: 8), [P8, K6, T2L] to last 10(13: 16) sts, P8, K to end.
3rd row P 2(5: 8), [K8, P1, T2L, P5] to last 10(13: 16) sts, K8, P to end.
4th row K 2(5: 8), [P8, K4, T2L, K2] to last 10(13: 16) sts, P8, K to end.
5th row P 2(5: 8), [C8, P3, T2L, P3] to last 10(13: 16) sts, C8, P to end.
6th row K 2(5: 8), [P8, K2, T2L, K4] to last 10(13: 16) sts, P8, K to end.
7th row P 2(5: 8), [K8, P5, T2L, P1] to last 10(13: 16) sts, K8, P to end.
8th row K 2(5: 8), [P8, T2L, K6] to last 10(13: 16) sts, P8, K to end.
9th row P 2(5: 8), [C8, P6, T2R] to last 10(13: 16) sts, C8, P to end.
10th row K 2(5: 8), [P8, K1, T2R, K5] to last 10(13: 16) sts, P8, K to end.
11th row P 2(5: 8), [K8, P4, T2R, P2] to last 10(13: 16) sts, K8, P to end.
12th row K 2(5: 8), [P8, K3, T2R, K3] to last 10(13: 16) sts, P8, K to end.
13th row P 2(5: 8), [K8, P2, T2R, P4] to last 10(13: 16) sts, K8, P to end.
14th row K 2(5: 8), [P8, K5, T2R, K1] to last 10(13: 16) sts, P8, K to end.
15th row P 2(5: 8), [K8, T2R, P6] to last 10(13: 16) sts, K8, P to end.
Rows 2–15 form the rep of patt. Cont until work meas 73 cm (28¾ ins) from beg, ending with a WS row.

Shape Shoulders

Keeping patt correct, cast off 15(16: 16) sts at beg of next 6 rows, then 16(15: 17) sts at beg of foll 2 rows.
Cast off rem 50(52: 54) sts.

POCKET LININGS (make 3)

With 3¾ mm (No. 9/US 4) needles cast on 35 sts.
Work 9 cm (3½ ins) in rib as for Back welt, ending with a WS row and inc one st in centre of last row. 36 sts.
Leave sts on a holder.

LEFT FRONT

With 3¼ mm (No. 10/US 3) needles cast on 69(71: 75) sts and work 6 cm (2¼ ins) in rib as for Back welt, ending with a RS row.
Inc row Rib 13 and sl these sts on to a safety pin, [rib 2, m1] 27(28: 27) times, rib to end. 83(86: 89) sts.
Change to 4 mm (No. 8/US 5) needles and cont in patt as folls:
1st row P 2(5: 8), [K9, P7] to last st, P1.
2nd row K1, [K6, T2L, P8] to last 2(5: 8) sts, K to end.
3rd row P 2(5: 8), [K8, P1, T2L, P5] to last st, P1.
4th row K1, [K4, T2L, K2, P8] to last 2(5: 8) sts, K to end.
This sets position of patt. Cont to match Back until work meas 15 cm (6 ins) from beg, ending with a WS row.

* Place Pocket

Next row Patt 28(31: 34), sl next 36 sts on to a holder, with RS facing patt to end across sts of one pocket lining, patt to end. *
Cont until work meas 45 cm (17¾ ins) from beg, ending with a WS row.
Rep from * to * once more.
Cont until work meas 70 cm (27½ ins) from beg, ending with a RS row.

Shape Neck

Keeping patt correct, cast off 9(10: 11) sts at beg of next row, then 4 sts at beg of foll 3 alt rows.
Dec one st at end of next row. 61(63: 65) sts.
Cont without shaping until work meas same as Back to shoulders, ending with a WS row.

Shape Shoulder

Keeping patt correct, cast off 15(16: 16) sts at beg of next and foll 2 alt rows. Work 1 row straight, then cast off rem 16(15: 17) sts.

RIGHT FRONT

With 3¼ mm (No. 10/US 3) needles cast on 69(71: 75) sts and work 4 rows in rib as for Back welt.
Next row Rib 5, cast off 4 sts, rib to end.
Next row Rib to end, casting on 4 sts over the 4 cast off.
Cont in rib as set until work meas 6 cm (2¼ ins) from beg, ending with a RS row.
Inc row Rib 2(2: 8), m1, [rib 2, m1] 26(27: 26) times, rib 2, turn and leave rem 13 sts on a safety pin. 83(86: 89) sts.
Change to 4 mm (No. 8/US 5) needles and cont in patt as folls:
1st row P1, [K1, P7, K8] to last 2(5: 8) sts, P to end.
2nd row K 2(5: 8), [P8, K6, T2L] to last st, K1.
3rd row P1, [P1, T2L, P5, K8] to last 2(5: 8) sts, P to end.
4th row K 2(5: 8), [P8, K4, T2L, K2] to last st, K1.
This sets position of patt. Cont to match Back until work meas 15 cm (6 ins) from beg, ending with a WS row.

Place Pocket

Next row Patt 19, sl next 36 sts on to a holder, with RS facing patt to end across sts of 3rd pocket lining, patt to end.
Cont to match Left Front, reversing all shaping and omitting top pocket.

SLEEVES

With 3¼ mm (No. 10/US 3) needles cast on 57 sts and work 6 cm (2¼ ins) in rib as for Back welt, ending with a RS row.
Inc row Rib 3, m1, [rib 1, m1, rib 2, m1] 17 times, rib 3. 92 sts.
Change to 4 mm (No. 8/US 5) needles.
Cont in patt as for first size on Back, *at the same time*, inc one st at each end of the 5th and every foll 4th row, working inc sts into patt until there are 152 sts.
Cont without shaping until work meas 48 cm (19 ins) from beg, ending with a WS row.
Cast off *loosely*.

COLLAR

With 3¼ mm (No. 10/US 3) needles cast on 133(137: 141) sts.
Work 12 cm (4¾ ins) in rib as for Back welt.
Cast off in rib.

BUTTON BAND

With 3¼ mm (No. 10/US 3) needles and RS facing rib to end across sts on safety pin at beg of left front, working twice into first st. 14 sts.
Cont in rib as set until band, when slightly stretched, reaches up front edge to neck.
Cast off in rib.
Tack band in place; with pins mark position of buttons, first to come level with buttonhole already worked, 2nd to come 1 cm (½ in) from cast-off edge, with 6 more spaced evenly between these 2.

BUTTONHOLE BAND

With 3¼ mm (No. 10/US 3) needles and WS facing rib to end across sts on safety pin at beg of right front, working twice into first st. 14 sts.
Cont to match Button Band, making buttonholes to correspond with positions of pins as folls:
(RS) Rib 5, cast off 4 sts, rib 5.
Next row Rib to end, casting on 4 sts over the 4 cast off.

POCKET TOPS

With 3¼ mm (No. 10/US 3) needles and RS facing, K to end across sts on holder dec 3 sts evenly across them. 33 sts.
Beg with a 2nd row, work 7 rows in rib as for Back welt.
Cast off in rib.

TO MAKE UP

Do not press.
Join shoulder seams. Sew in sleeves, with centre of sleeve to shoulder seam. Join side and sleeve seams. Sew down pocket tops and pocket linings. Sew on front bands. Sew cast-off edge of collar to neck edge.
Press seams lightly on WS according to instructions on ball band, omitting ribbing. Sew on buttons.

SKIRT

BACK AND FRONT (alike)

With 3¾ mm (No. 9/US 4) needles cast on 123(131: 139) sts and work 4 cm (1½ ins) in rib as for Back welt of Jacket, ending with a RS row.
Inc row Rib 1(8: 9), m1, [rib 2, m1, rib 3, m1] 24(23: 24) times, rib to end. 172(178: 188) sts.
Change to 4 mm (No. 8/US 5) needles.
Cont in patt as for 1st(2nd: 1st) size on Back of Jacket until work meas 34 cm (13½ ins) from beg, ending with a WS row.

Shape Sides
Keeping patt correct, dec one st at each end of next and every foll 4th row until 140(148: 156) sts rem.
Cont without shaping until work meas 56 cm (22 ins) from beg, ending with a WS row.
Cast off, working [K2 tog] 4 times across each cable.

TO MAKE UP

Do not press.
Join side seams. Join ends of elastic to form a circle, place inside cast-off edge and sew in position using a herringbone casing.
Press seams lightly on WS according to instructions on ball band, omitting ribbing.

SAILOR-COLLARED CARDIGAN
WITH LACE TRIM

BACK

With 3¼ mm (No. 10/US 3) needles cast on 105(112: 119: 147: 154: 161) sts.
Beg with a P row, work 5 rows in st st.
6th row (RS) K2, [K2 tog, yfwd, K5] to last 5 sts, K2 tog, yfwd, K3.
Beg with a P row, work 5 rows in st st.
12th row K5, [K2 tog, yfwd, K5] to last 2 sts, K2.
Rep these 12 rows until work meas 15(17: 19: 21: 22: 23) cm [6(6¾: 7½: 8¼: 8¾: 9) ins] from beg, ending with a P row.

Shape Armholes

Keeping patt correct cast off 6(7: 7: 9: 9: 10) sts at beg of next 2 rows.
Dec one st at each end of next 5 rows, then every foll alt row until 79(84: 89: 107: 112: 117) sts rem.
Cont without shaping until work meas 30(33: 36: 42: 44: 46) cm [11¾(13: 14¼: 16½: 17¼: 18) ins] from beg, ending with a P row.

Shape Shoulder and Neck

Next row Cast off 8(8: 9: 11: 12: 13) sts, patt 19(21: 22: 27: 28: 29) including st already on needle after casting off, cast off 25(26: 27: 31: 32: 33) sts, patt to end.
Cont on last set of sts only:
Next row Cast off 8(8: 9: 11: 12: 13) sts, patt to end.
Next row Cast off 2 sts, patt to end.
Rep the last 2 rows once more.
Cast off rem 7(9: 9: 12: 12: 12) sts.
Return to sts that were left; with WS facing rejoin yarn to neck edge, cast off 2 sts and patt to end.
Cont to match first side, reversing all shaping.

LEFT FRONT

With 3¼ mm (No. 10/US 3) needles cast on 48(52: 55: 69: 73: 76) sts.
Beg with a P row, work 5 rows in st st. **
6th row (RS) K5, [K2 tog, yfwd, K5] to last 1(5: 1: 5: 1: 5) sts, [K2 tog, yfwd] 0(1: 0: 1: 0: 1) time, K to end.

MATERIALS

5(6: 8: 13: 13: 14) 50 g balls of Rowan Cabled Mercerised Cotton.
1 pair each of 2¼ mm (No. 13/US 0) and 3¼ mm (No. 10/US 3) knitting needles.
6(6: 6: 7: 7: 7) buttons.

MEASUREMENTS

To fit Chest/ Bust	61 cm (66: 71: 86: 91: 97)	24 ins (26: 28: 34: 36: 38)
All round approx.	69 cm (74: 79: 97: 102: 107)	27 ins (29: 31: 38: 40: 42)
Length to shoulder	35 cm (38: 41: 47: 49: 51)	13¾ ins (15: 16¼: 18½: 19¼: 20)
Sleeve seam	28 cm (32: 36: 47: 48: 49)	11 ins (12½: 14¼: 18½: 19: 19¼)

TENSION

30 sts and 42 rows to 10 cm (4 ins) over eyelet patt using 3¼ mm (No. 10/US 3) needles.

ABBREVIATIONS

See page 10.

Beg with a P row, work 5 rows in st st.
12th row K2, [K2 tog, yfwd, K5] to last 4(1: 4: 1: 4: 1) sts, [K2 tog, yfwd] 1(0: 1: 0: 1: 0) time, K to end.
These 12 rows form the rep of patt.
Cont until work meas same as Back to armholes, ending with a P row.

Shape Armhole and Front Edge

Keeping patt correct, cast off 6(7: 7: 9: 9: 10) sts at beg of next row and 3 sts at beg of foll row.

Dec one st at armhole edge on next 5 rows. Work 1 row straight.
Dec one st at beg of next and foll 1(1: 2: 5: 6: 6) alt rows, *at the same time*, dec one st at front edge on next and every foll 5th row until 30(33: 31: 42: 43: 47) sts rem.
Keeping armhole edge straight, cont to dec at front edge only on every foll 5th(5th: 6th: 6th: 6th: 6th) row until 23(25: 27: 34: 36: 38) sts rem.
Cont without shaping until work meas same as Back to shoulders, ending with a P row.

Shape Shoulder

Cast off 8(9: 9: 11: 12: 13) sts at beg of next and foll alt row. Work 1 row straight, then cast off rem 7(9: 9: 12: 12: 12) sts.

RIGHT FRONT

Work as given for Left Front to **.
6th row (RS) K 5(2: 5: 2: 5: 2), [K2 tog, yfwd, K5] to last st, K1.
Beg with a P row, work 5 rows in st st.
12th row K 1(5: 1: 5: 1: 5), [K2 tog, yfwd, K5] to last 5 sts, K2 tog, yfwd, K to end.
This sets position of patt. Cont to match Left Front, reversing all shaping.

SLEEVES

With 3¼ mm (No. 10/US 3) needles cast on 55(59: 62: 66: 69: 73) sts.
Cont in patt as given for 1st(2nd: 1st: 2nd: 1st: 2nd) size Left Front, *at the same time*, inc one st at each end of the 7th and every foll 6th row, working inc sts into patt until there are 81(87: 96: 118: 123: 129) sts.
Cont without shaping until work meas 23(27: 31: 42: 43: 44) cm [9(10¾: 12¼: 16½: 17: 17¼) ins] from beg, ending with a P row.

Shape Top
Keeping patt correct cast off 6(7: 7: 9: 9: 10) sts at beg of next 2 rows.
Dec one st at each end of next and every foll alt row until 55(55: 60: 62: 63: 63) sts rem, then at each end of every row until 21(23: 24: 26: 27: 27) sts rem.
Cast off.

COLLAR

With 3¼ mm (No. 10/US 3) needles cast on 61(64: 67: 77: 80: 83) sts.
Beg with a K row, cont in st st until work meas 11(11: 11: 15: 15: 15) cm [4¼(4¼: 4¼: 6: 6: 6) ins] from beg, ending with a K row.

Shape Neck
Next row P 18(19: 20: 23: 24: 25), cast off 25(26: 27: 31: 32: 33) sts, P to end.
Cont on last set of sts only:
K 1 row.
Cast off 2 sts at beg of next and foll alt row.
Dec one st at end of 13th(13th: 13th: 15th: 15th: 15th) and every foll 6th row until 12(13: 14: 14: 15: 16) sts rem.

Work 3 rows straight.
Dec one st at end of next and every foll 4th row until 2 sts rem. Work 2 rows straight, then P2 tog and fasten off.
Return to sts which were left; with RS facing rejoin yarn to neck edge, cast off 2 sts and K to end.
Cont to match first side, reversing all shaping.

BUTTON BAND

With 2¼ mm (No. 13/US 0) needles cast on 9 sts.
Work in garter st until band, when slightly stretched, fits up left front edge to beg of shaping.
Cast off.
Tack band in place; with pins mark position of buttons, first to come 1 cm (½ in) from lower edge, 2nd to come 2 cm (¾ in) from cast off edge, with 4(4: 4: 5: 5: 5) more spaced evenly between these 2.

BUTTONHOLE BAND

Work as given for Button Band, making buttonholes to correspond with positions of pins as folls:
(RS) K3, cast off 3 sts, K3.
Next row K to end, casting on 3 sts over the 3 cast off.

CUFFS

With 2¼ mm (No. 13/US 0) needles cast on 12 sts.
1st row (WS) K4, yfwd, sl 1, K2 tog, psso, yfwd, K3, yfwd, K2.
2nd row K4, [K1, P1, K1, P1, K1, P1] all into next st, P2, K6.
3rd row K4, yfwd, sl 1, K1, psso, K2 tog, cast off 5 sts, K3, yfwd, K2.
4th row K5, yfwd, K1, P1, K6.
5th row K4, yfwd, sl 1, K2 tog, psso, yfwd, K3, yfwd, K2 tog, yfwd, K2.
6th row K6, [K1, P1, K1, P1, K1, P1] all into next st, P2, K6.
7th row K4, yfwd, sl 1, K1, psso, K2 tog, cast off 5 sts, K3, yfwd, K2 tog, yfwd, K2.
8th row Cast off 4 sts, K3, yfwd, K1, P1, K6.
These 8 rows form the rep of patt.
Cont until cuff, when slightly

stretched, fits along lower edge of sleeve, ending with an 8th patt row.
Cast off.

WELT

Join side seams. Sew on front bands.
With 2¼ mm (No. 13/US 0) needles cast on 12 sts and work 4 rows in garter st.
Work in patt as given for Cuffs until band, when slightly stretched, fits along lower edge of back and fronts, ending with an 8th patt row.
Work 4 rows in garter st.
Cast off.

COLLAR EDGING

With 2¼ mm (No. 13/US 0) needles cast on 12 sts.
Work in patt as given for Cuffs until edging, when slightly stretched, fits along outside edge of collar to 1 cm (½ in) before first corner, ending with a 1st patt row.
* **Next row** Patt to last 3 sts, yfwd, sl 1, yb, turn.
Next row Sl 1, yb, patt to end.
Next row Patt to end.
Next row Patt to end. *
Rep from * to * 5 times more. **
Cont in patt as set until edging, when slightly stretched, fits along cast on edge of collar to 1 cm (½ in) before 2nd corner, ending with a 1st patt row.
Rep from * to ** once more.
Cont in patt as set until edging, when slightly stretched, fits along outside edge, ending with an 8th patt row.
Cast off.

TO MAKE UP

Press work lightly on WS according to instructions on ball band, omitting edgings.
Join shoulder seams. Sew in sleeves. Sew straight edge of cuffs to sleeves. Join sleeve seams. Sew straight edge of welt to lower edge of back and fronts, beginning and ending at front edge of bands. Sew straight edge of collar edging in place. Sew collar to neck edge, sewing ends of collar to cast off sts at centre front and edging to top of front bands.
Press seams. Sew on buttons.

JACQUARD SHAWL-COLLARED SWEATER

MATERIALS

7(8) 50 g balls of Hayfield Pure
Wool Classics DK in main colour,
M.
5 balls in first contrast colour, A.
2 balls in each of 2nd and 3rd
contrast colours, B and C.
1 ball in each of 4th, 5th and 6th
contrast colours, D, E and F.
1 pair each of 3¼ mm (No. 10/US 3)
and 4 mm (No. 8/US 5) knitting
needles.
3¼ mm (No. 10/US 3) circular
needle, 60 cm OR 24 ins long.

MEASUREMENTS

To fit Bust/	86–91 cm	34–36 ins
Chest	(102–107)	(40–42)
Actual	119 cm	47 ins
measure-	(129)	(51)
ment		
Length to	70 cm	27½ ins
shoulder	(71)	(28)
Sleeve seam	49 cm	19¼ ins
	(51)	(20)

TENSION

22 sts and 28 rows to 10 cm (4 ins)
over st st using 4 mm (No. 8/US 5)
needles.

ABBREVIATIONS

See page 10.

NOTE

When working patt from Chart,
read odd rows (K) from right to left
and even rows (P) from left to
right. Use a separate length of yarn
for each section and twist yarns tog
where they join on every row to
avoid a hole. When working rows
4–11 from Chart, strand yarn not in
use *loosely* across WS of work to
keep fabric elastic.

BACK

With 3¼ mm (No. 10/US 3) needles and
A, cast on 126(134) sts.
1st row (RS) K2, [P2, K2] to end.
2nd row P2, [K2, P2] to end.
Rep these 2 rows until work meas
10 cm (4 ins) from beg, ending with a
WS row and inc 7(9) sts evenly across
the last row. 133(143) sts.
Change to 4 mm (No. 8/US 5) needles.
Beg with a K row and working in st st
throughout, cont in patt from Chart
starting and ending rows as indicated
until 98(102) rows in all have been
worked in st st.

Shape Armholes

Cast off 5 sts at beg of next 2 rows.
123(133) sts.
Cont without shaping until 168(172)
rows in all have been worked in st st.

Shape Shoulders

Cast off 14(16) sts at beg of next 4
rows, then 15(16) sts at beg of foll 2
rows.
Leave rem 37 sts on a holder for collar.

KEY

☐ M
■ A
☒ B
• C
◺ D
△ E
◯ F

BACK, FRONT AND SLEEVES

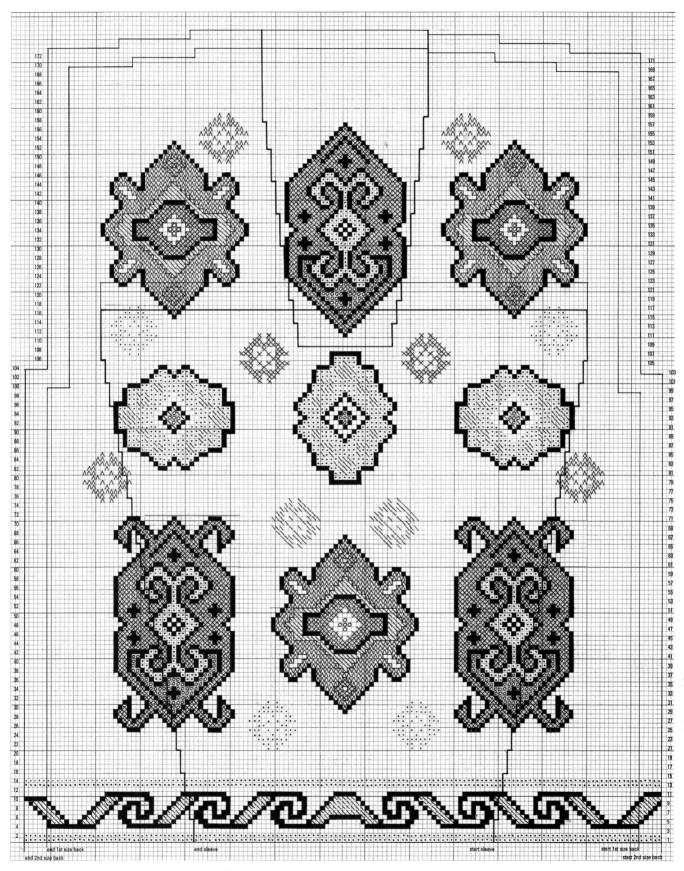

FRONT

Work as given for Back until 108 rows in all have been worked in st st.

Shape Neck
Next row Patt 51(56), cast off 21 sts, patt to end.
Cont on last set of sts only;
Dec one st at neck edge on the 5th and every foll 5th row until 48(53) sts rem, then every foll 7th row until 43(48) sts rem.
Cont without shaping until 169(173) rows in all have been worked in st st.

Shape Shoulder
Cast off 14(16) sts at beg of next and foll alt row. Work 1 row straight, then cast off rem 15(16) sts.
Return to sts that were left; with WS facing rejoin M to neck edge and patt to end.
Cont to match first side, reversing all shaping.

SLEEVES

With 3¼ mm (No. 10/US 3) needles and A, cast on 54 sts and work 10 cm (4 ins) in rib as for Back welt, ending with a RS row.
Inc row Rib 3, m1, [rib 4, m1] 12 times, rib 3. 67 sts.
Change to 4 mm (No. 8/US 5) needles.
Beg with a K row and working in st st throughout, cont in patt from Chart starting and ending rows as indicated, *at the same time*, inc one st at each end of the 6th and every foll 5th row, working inc sts into patt until there are 109 sts.
Omitting part motifs, cont without shaping until 116(122) rows in all have been worked in st st.
Cast off *loosely*.

COLLAR

Join shoulder seams.
With 3¼ mm (No. 10/US 3) circular needle, A and RS facing, pick up and K 66(70) sts evenly up right front neck, K back neck sts from holder inc 11 sts evenly across them, then pick up and K 66(70) sts evenly down left front neck. 180(188) sts.
TURN and cont in ROWS:
1st row (WS) K1, [P2, K2] to last 3 sts, P2, K1.

2nd row P1, [K2, P2] to last 3 sts, K2, P1.
Rep these 2 rows until collar meas 10 cm (4 ins).
Cast of *loosely* in rib.

TO MAKE UP

Press work lightly on WS according to instructions on ball band, omitting ribbing.
Sew in sleeves, with last 6 rows to cast off sts at underarm. Join side and sleeve seams. Sew row ends of collar to cast off sts at centre front, crossing right over left.
Press seams.

TAPESTRY BIRD AND FLOWER SWEATER

FRONT

With 3¼ mm (No. 10/US 3) needles and M, cast on 111(115: 119) sts.
1st row (RS) K1, [P1, K1] to end.
2nd row P1, [K1, P1] to end.
Rep these 2 rows until work meas 8 cm (3¼ ins) from beg, ending with a RS row.
Inc row Rib 1(7: 5), m1, [rib 6(5: 5), m1] 18(20: 22) times, rib to end. 130(136: 142) sts.
Change to 4 mm (No. 8/US 5) needles **.
Beg with a K row and working in st st throughout, cont in patt from Chart starting and ending rows as indicated until 150 rows in all have been worked in st st.

Shape Neck

Next row Patt 53(56: 59), turn and leave rem sts on a spare needle.
Keeping patt correct, then working in M only when Chart is complete; dec one st at neck edge on next 7 rows, then every foll alt row until 44(47: 50) sts rem.
Cont without shaping until work meas 68 cm (26¾ ins) from beg, ending with a P row.
Cast off.
Return to sts on spare needle; with RS facing sl first 24 sts on to a holder for neckband, rejoin M to neck edge and patt to end.
Cont to match first side, reversing shaping.

BACK

Work as given for Front to **.
Beg with a K row, cont in st st until work meas same as Front to shoulders, ending with a P row.

Shape Shoulders

Cast off 44(47: 50) sts at beg of next 2 rows.
Leave rem 42 sts on a holder for neckband.

MATERIALS

12(13: 14) 50 g balls of Hayfield Pure Wool Classics DK in main colour, M.
1 ball in each of 9 contrast colours, A, B, C, D, E, F, G, H and J.
1 pair each of 3¼ mm (No. 10/US 3) and 4 mm (No. 8/US 5) knitting needles.

MEASUREMENTS

To fit Bust	86 cm (91: 97)	34 ins (36: 38)
Actual measurement	117 cm (122: 127)	46 ins (48: 50)
Length to shoulder	68 cm	26¾ ins
Sleeve seam	45 cm (46: 47)	17¾ ins (18: 18½)

TENSION

22 sts and 28 rows to 10 cm (4 ins) over st st using 4 mm (No. 8/US 5) needles.

ABBREVIATIONS

See page 10.

NOTE

When working patts from Chart, read odd rows (K) from right to left and even rows (P) from left to right. Use a separate length of yarn for each section and twist yarns tog where they join on every row to avoid a hole.

RIGHT SLEEVE

With 3¼ mm (No. 10/US 3) needles and M, cast on 49(51: 53) sts and work 8 cm (3¼ ins) in rib as for Front welt, ending with a RS row.
Inc row Rib 8(7: 6), m1, [rib 2, m1] 16(18: 20) times, rib to end. 66(70: 74) sts.

Change to 4 mm (No. 8/US 5) needles and cont in patt as folls:
Beg with a K row cont in st st, inc one st at each end of the 5th and every foll 4th row until there are 80(84: 88) sts. **.
Next row P 31(33: 35) M, 4B, 12M, 2A, 31(33: 35) M.
Next row K 31(33: 35) M, 2A, 11M, 7B, 29(31: 33) M.
Next row P 28(30: 32) M, 9B, 10M, 2A, 31(33: 35) M.
Next row Inc in first st, K 30(32: 34) M, 2A, 9M, 10B, 27(29: 31) M, inc in last st.
Next row P 29(31: 33) M, 11B, 8M, 2A, 32(34: 36) M.
Next row K 32(34: 36) M, 2A, 7M, 9B, 1M, 2B, 29(31: 33) M.
This sets position of motif. Beg on row 116 and keeping patt sts correct as marked between broken lines on left-hand side of Chart, cont in patt as set, *at the same time*, inc one st at each end of the 2nd and every foll 4th row until the 45 rows of patt are complete, then cont in M only until there are 110(114: 118) sts.
Cont without shaping until work meas 45(46: 47) cm [17¾(18: 18½) ins] from beg, ending with a P row.
Cast off *loosely*.

LEFT SLEEVE

Work as given for Right Sleeve to **.
Next row P 31(33: 35) M, 2A, 12M, 4B, 31(33: 35) M.
Next row K 29(31: 33) M, 7B, 11M, 2A, 31(33: 35) M.
Next row P 31(33: 35) M, 2A, 10M, 9B, 28(30: 32) M.
This sets position of motif. Cont to match Right Sleeve, reversing patt as set by working between broken lines on right-hand side of Chart, omitting part flowers as before.

BACK, FRONT AND SLEEVES

KEY

□	M	◿	E
◣	A	☑	F
◺	B	◹	G
•	C	◯	H
■	D	☒	J

NECKBAND

Join right shoulder seam.
With 3¼ mm (No. 10/US 3) needles, M
and RS facing, pick up and K 22 sts
evenly down left front neck, K front
neck sts from holder, pick up and
K 21 sts evenly up right front neck,
then K back neck sts from holder.
109 sts.
Beg with a 2nd row, work 7 cm (2¾ ins)
in rib as for Front welt.
Cast off *loosely* in rib.

TO MAKE UP

Press work lightly on WS according to
instructions on ball band, omitting
ribbing.
Join left shoulder and neckband seam.
Sew in sleeves, with centre of sleeve to
shoulder seam. Join side and sleeve
seams. Fold neckband in half to inside
and sl st.
Press seams.

FORTIES-STYLE TWINSET

CARDIGAN

BACK

With 2¾ mm (No. 12/US 1) needles cast on 107(113: 119) sts.
1st row (RS) P1, [K1, P1] to end.
2nd row K1, [P1, K1] to end.
Rep these 2 rows until work meas 10 cm (4 ins) from beg, ending with a WS row.
Inc row Rib 4, m1, [rib 3, m1] 33(35: 37) times, rib 4. 141(149: 157) sts.
Change to 3¼ mm (No. 10/US 3) needles and cont in patt as folls:
1st and every foll alt row (WS) K 11(15: 12), [P7, K7] to last 4(8: 5) sts, K to end.
2nd row K 4(8: 5), [K11, K2 tog, yfwd, K1] to last 11(15: 12) sts, K to end.
4th row K 4(8: 5), [K10, K2 tog, yfwd, K2] to last 11(15: 12) sts, K to end.
6th row K 4(8: 5), [K9, K2 tog, yfwd, K3] to last 11(15: 12) sts, K to end.
8th row K 4(8: 5), [K8, K2 tog, yfwd, K4] to last 11(15: 12) sts, K to end.
10th row K 4(8: 5), [K7, K2 tog, yfwd, K5] to last 11(15: 12) sts, K to end.
12th row K 4(8: 5), [K8, yfwd, K2 tog, K4] to last 11(15: 12) sts, K to end.
14th row K 4(8: 5), [K9, yfwd, K2 tog, K3] to last 11(15: 12) sts, K to end.
16th row K 4(8: 5), [K10, yfwd, K2 tog, K2] to last 11(15: 12) sts, K to end.
18th row K 4(8: 5), [K11, yfwd, K2 tog, K1] to last 11(15: 12) sts, K to end.
20th row K 4(8: 5), [K12, yfwd, K2 tog] to last 11(15: 12) sts, K to end.
These 20 rows form the rep of patt.
Cont until work meas 30(31: 32) cm [11¾(12¼: 12½) ins] from beg, ending with a WS row.

Shape Armholes
Keeping patt correct cast off 8(9: 10) sts at beg of next 2 rows.

MATERIALS

CARDIGAN: 7(8: 8) 50 g balls of Hayfield Pure Wool Classics 4 ply.
TOP: 4(4: 5) balls.
1 pair each of 2¾ mm (No. 12/US 1) and 3¼ mm (No. 10/US 3) knitting needles.
7 buttons for Cardigan and 3 buttons for Top.

MEASUREMENTS

To fit Bust	86 cm	34 ins
	(91: 97)	(36: 38)
CARDIGAN:		
All round	99 cm	39 ins
approx.	(107: 112)	(42: 44)
Length to	49 cm	19¼ ins
shoulder	(51: 53)	(20: 20¾)
Sleeve seam	44 cm	17¼ ins
	(45: 46)	(17¾: 18)
TOP:		
All round	91 cm	36 ins
approx.	(97: 102)	(38: 40)
Length to	47 cm	18½ ins
shoulder	(48: 49)	(19: 19¼)

TENSION

28 sts and 42 rows to 10 cm (4 ins) over patt using 3¼ mm (No. 10/ US 3) needles.

ABBREVIATIONS

See page 10.

Dec one st at each end of next and every foll alt row until 107(113: 119) sts rem.
Cont without shaping until work meas 49(51: 53) cm [19¼(20: 20¾) ins] from beg, ending with a WS row.

Shape Shoulders
Keeping patt correct, cast off 11(11: 12) sts at beg of next 2 rows, 11(12: 12) sts at beg of foll 2 rows, then 11(12: 13) sts at beg of next 2 rows.
Leave rem 41(43: 45) sts on a holder for neckband.

LEFT FRONT

With 2¾ mm (No. 12/US 1) needles cast on 51(53: 57) sts and work 10 cm (4 ins) in rib as for Back welt, ending with a WS row.
Inc row Rib 3(1: 2), m1, [rib 3, m1] 15(17: 18) times, rib to end. 67(71: 76) sts.
Change to 3¼ mm (No. 10/US 3) needles and cont in patt as folls: **
1st and every foll alt row (WS) K 7(7: 1), [P7, K7] 4(4: 5) times, K to end.
2nd row K 4(8: 5), [K11, K2 tog, yfwd, K1] 4(4: 5) times, K to end.
4th row K 4(8: 5), [K10, K2 tog, yfwd, K2] 4(4: 5) times, K to end.
This sets position of patt. Cont to match Back until work meas same as Back to armholes, ending with a WS row.

Shape Armhole
Keeping patt correct, cast off 8(9: 10) sts at beg of next row. Work 1 row straight.
Dec one st at beg of next and every foll alt row until 50(53: 57) sts rem.
Cont without shaping until work meas 39(41: 43) cm [15¼(16¼: 17) ins] from beg, ending with a RS row.

Shape Neck
Keeping patt correct, cast off 6 sts at beg of next row, 4 sts at beg of foll alt row, then 2 sts at beg of next alt row.
Dec one st at neck edge on next and every foll alt row until 33(35: 37) sts rem.
Cont without shaping until work meas same as Back to shoulders, ending with a WS row.

Shape Shoulder
Keeping patt correct, cast off 11(11: 12) sts at beg of next row and 11(12: 12) sts at beg of foll alt row. Work 1 row straight, then cast off rem 11(12: 13) sts.

RIGHT FRONT

Work as given for Left Front to **.
1st and every foll alt row (WS) K 4(8: 5), [K7, P7] 4(4: 5) times, K to end.
2nd row K 7(7: 1), [K4, K2 tog, yfwd, K8] 4(4: 5) times, K to end.
This sets position of patt. Cont to match Left Front, reversing all shaping.

SLEEVES

With 2¾ mm (No. 12/US 1) needles cast on 55(57: 59) sts and work 10 cm (4 ins) in rib as for Back welt, ending with a WS row.
Inc row Rib 6(1: 2), m1, [rib 4(5: 5), m1] 11 times, rib to end. 67(69: 71) sts.
Change to 3¼ mm (No. 10/US 3) needles and cont in patt as folls:
1st row (WS) P 2(3: 4), K7, [P7, K7] to last 2(3: 4) sts, P to end.
2nd row K 2(3: 4), [K11, K2 tog, yfwd, K1] to last 9(10: 11) sts, K to end.
This sets position of patt. Cont to match Back, *at the same time*, inc one st at each end of the 5th and every foll 8th row, working inc sts into patt until there are 99(103: 107) sts.
Cont without shaping until work meas 44(45: 46) cm [17¼(17¾: 18) ins] from beg, ending with a WS row.

Shape Top
Keeping patt correct cast off 8(9: 10) sts at beg of next 2 rows.
Dec one st at each end of next and every foll alt row until 37 sts rem.
Cast off.

NECKBAND

Join shoulder seams.
With 2¾ mm (No. 12/US 1) needles and RS facing, pick up and K 42(43: 44) sts evenly up right front neck, K back neck sts from holder, then pick up and K 42(43: 44) sts evenly down left front neck. 125(129: 133) sts.
Beg with a 2nd row, work 11 rows in rib as for Back welt.
Cast off in rib.

BUTTONHOLE BAND

With 2¾ mm (No. 12/US 1) needles and RS facing, pick up and K 127(133: 139) sts evenly up right front edge to top of neckband.
Work 4 rows in rib as for Back welt.
Next row Rib 5, cast off 3 sts, [rib 16(17: 18), cast off 3 sts] 6 times, rib 5.
Next row Rib to end, casting on 3 sts over each 3 cast off.
Work 5 more rows, then cast off *loosely* in rib as set.

BUTTON BAND

Work to match Buttonhole Band, omitting buttonholes.

TO MAKE UP

Do not press.
Sew in sleeves. Join side and sleeve seams.
Press seams lightly on WS according to instructions on ball band, omitting ribbing. Sew on buttons.

TOP

BACK

With 2¾ mm (No. 12/US 1) needles cast on 91(97: 103) sts and work 10 cm (4 ins) in rib as for Back welt of Cardigan, ending with a WS row.
Inc row Rib 10(11: 12), m1, [rib 2, m1] 35(37: 39) times, rib to end. 127(135: 143) sts.
Change to 3¼ mm (No. 10/US 3) needles.
Cont in patt as for Back of Cardigan until work meas 31 cm (12¼ ins) from beg, ending with a WS row. **

Shape Armholes
Keeping patt correct cast off 6(7: 8) sts at beg of next 2 rows.
Dec one st at each end of next and every foll alt row until 109(115: 121) sts rem.
Cont without shaping until work meas 47(48: 49) cm [18½(19: 19¼) ins] from beg, ending with a WS row.

Shape Shoulders

Keeping patt correct, cast off 12(12: 13) sts at beg of next 2 rows, 12(13: 13) sts at beg of foll 2 rows, then 12(13: 14) sts at beg of next 2 rows.
Leave rem 37(39: 41) sts on a holder for collar.

FRONT

Work as given for Back to **.

Shape Armholes and Divide for Opening

Next row Cast off 6(7: 8) sts, patt 54(57: 60) including st already on needle after casting off, cast off 7 sts, patt to end.
Cont on last set of sts only:
Next row Cast off 6(7: 8) sts, patt to end.
Keeping front edge straight, dec one st at end of next and foll 2 alt rows. 51(54: 57) sts.
Cont without shaping until work meas 41(42: 43) cm [16¼(16½: 17) ins] from beg, ending with a WS row.

Shape Neck

Keeping patt correct, cast off 6(7: 8) sts at beg of next row.
Dec one st at neck edge on next 7 rows, then every foll alt row until 36(38: 40) sts rem.
Cont without shaping until work meas same as Back to shoulders, ending with a RS row.

Shape Shoulder

Keeping patt correct, cast off 12(12: 13) sts at beg of next row and 12(13: 13) sts at beg of foll alt row. Work 1 row straight, then cast off rem 12(13: 14) sts.
Return to sts that were left; with WS facing rejoin yarn and patt to end.
Cont to match first side, reversing all shaping.

ARMHOLE BORDERS

Join shoulder seams.
With 2¾ mm (No. 12/US 1) needles and RS facing, pick up and K 121(127:

133) sts evenly around armhole edge.
Work 3 cm (1¼ ins) in rib as for Back welt of Cardigan.
Cast off in rib.

BUTTON BAND

With 2¾ mm (No. 12/US 1) needles and RS facing, pick up and K 33(35: 39) sts evenly down left front opening.
Work 16 rows in garter st.
Cast off knitwise.

BUTTONHOLE BAND

With 2¾ mm (No. 12/US 1) needles and RS facing, pick up and K 33(35: 39) sts evenly up right front opening.
Work 4 rows in garter st.
* **Next 2 rows** K 11(11: 13), turn, K2 tog tbl, K 7(7: 9), K2 tog.
Next 2 rows K 9(9: 11), turn, K2 tog tbl, K 5(5: 7), K2 tog.
Next 2 rows K 7(7: 9), turn, K2 tog tbl, K 1(1: 2), yfwd, K2 tog, K 0(0: 1), K2 tog.
Next 2 rows K 5(5: 7), turn, K2 tog tbl, K 1(1: 3), K2 tog.
Next row [K2 tog tbl] 0(0: 1) time, K 3(3: 1), [K2 tog] 0(0: 1) time.
Next row Sl 1, K2 tog, psso and fasten off.
Break off yarn. **
Return to sts that were left; with WS facing rejoin yarn to next st, cast off 0(1: 0) st. *
Rep from * to * once more, then from * to ** once again.

COLLAR

With 2¾ mm (No. 12/US 1) needles and RS facing, pick up and K 40(41: 42) sts evenly up right front neck beginning at base of first point, K back neck sts from holder, then pick up and K 40(41: 42) sts evenly down left front neck ending on 5th row of button band. 117(121: 125) sts.
Work 3 rows in garter st.
Inc row K 8(8: 7), m1, [K 4(5: 4), m1] 25(21: 28) times, K to end. 143(143: 154) sts.

Work 14 rows in garter st.
* **Next 2 rows** K11, turn, K2 tog tbl, K7, K2 tog.
Next 2 rows K9, turn, K2 tog tbl, K5, K2 tog.
Next 2 rows K7, turn, K2 tog tbl, K3, K2 tog.
Next 2 rows K5, turn, K2 tog tbl, K1, K2 tog.
Next row K3.
Next row Sl 1, K2 tog, psso and fasten off.
Break off yarn. **
Return to sts that were left; with WS facing rejoin yarn to next st. *
Rep from * to * 11(11: 12) times more, then from * to ** once again.

TO MAKE UP

Do not press.
Join side seams and ends of armhole borders. Sew ends of front bands to cast off sts at centre front.
Press seams lightly on WS according to instructions on ball band, omitting ribbing. Sew on buttons.

JACOBEAN TAPESTRY
SWEATER

FRONT

With 3¼ mm (No. 10/US 3) needles and
M, cast on 134 sts.
1st row (RS) K2, [P2, K2] to end.
2nd row P2, [K2, P2] to end.
Rep these 2 rows until work meas
10 cm (4 ins) from beg, ending with a
WS row.
Change to 4 mm (No. 8/US 5)
needles. **
Beg with a K row and working in st st
throughout, cont in patt from Chart
reading odd rows (K) from right to
left and even rows (P) from left to
right, until 158 rows in all have been
worked in st st.

Shape Neck
Next row Patt 56, turn and leave rem
sts on a spare needle.
Keeping patt correct cast off 4 sts at
beg of next row.
Dec one st at neck edge on next
5 rows, then every foll alt row until
43 sts rem.
Cont without shaping until 180 rows
in all have been worked in st st.
Cast off.
Return to sts on spare needle; with RS
facing sl first 22 sts on to a holder for
collar, rejoin M to neck edge, cast off
4 sts and patt to end.
Cont to match first side, reversing
shaping.

BACK

Work as given for Front to **.
Beg with a K row and working in st st
throughout, cont in patt from Chart
reading odd rows (K) from left to
right and even rows (P) from right to
left, thus reversing patt until 180 rows
in all have been worked in st st.

Shape Shoulders
Cast off 43 sts at beg of next 2 rows.
Leave rem 48 sts on a holder for collar.

MATERIALS

11 × 50 g balls of Hayfield Pure
Wool Classics DK in main colour,
M.
2 balls in each of 2 contrast colours,
A and B.
1 ball in each of 6 other contrast
colours, C, D, E, F, G and H.
1 pair each of 3¼ mm (No. 10/US 3)
and 4 mm (No. 8/US 5) knitting
needles.
Set of four 3¼ mm (No. 10/US 3)
double-pointed needles.

MEASUREMENTS

To fit Bust	86–97 cm	34–38 ins
Actual measurement	122 cm	48 ins
Length to shoulder	74 cm	29¼ ins
Sleeve with cuff back	49 cm	19¼ ins

TENSION

22 sts and 28 rows to 10 cm (4 ins)
over st st using 4 mm (No. 8/US 5)
needles.

ABBREVIATIONS

See page 10.

NOTE

When working patt from Charts
use a separate length of yarn for
each section and twist yarns tog
where they join on every row to
avoid a hole.

SLEEVES

With 3¼ mm (No. 10/US 3) needles and
M, cast on 54 sts and work 12 cm
(4¾ ins) in rib as for Front welt, ending
with a RS row.

Inc row Rib 4, m1, [rib 5, m1] 9 times,
rib 5. 64 sts.
Change to 4 mm (No. 8/US 5) needles.
Beg with a K row and working in st st
throughout, cont in patt from Chart
starting and ending rows as indicated,
read odd rows (K) from right to left
and even rows (P) from left to right, *at
the same time*, inc one st at each end of
the 5th and every foll 4th row,
working inc sts into patt until there are
102 sts, then every foll 5th row until
there are 110 sts.
Cont without shaping until 122 rows
in all have been worked in st st.
Cast off *loosely*.

COLLAR

Join shoulder seams.
With set of four 3¼ mm (No. 10/US 3)
needles, M and RS facing, pick up and
K 24 sts evenly down left front neck,
K front neck sts from holder inc 2 sts
evenly across them, pick up and
K 24 sts evenly up right front neck,
then K back neck sts from holder inc
4 sts evenly across them. 124 sts.
Work 18 cm (7 ins) in rounds of K2,
P2 rib.
Cast off *loosely* in rib.

TO MAKE UP

Press work lightly on WS according to
instructions on ball band, omitting
ribbing.
Sew in sleeves, with centre of sleeve to
shoulder seam.
Using A, B, D, E and F, work
embroidery to motifs using Chart as a
guide:
Work in Trellis st across solid H
section of large centre flower on back
and front and top right flower on
sleeves: lay B across space as required
to form a lattice patt, then with E
work a small cross st at each
intersection.
With D and A, work in Stem st around

outer edge of this same area.
With F, work 6 French Knots on M
centre of top 2 large flowers on back
and front and top left flower on
sleeves, wrapping yarn 3 times round
needle.
Join side and sleeve seams, reversing
seam on cuffs to allow for turning.
Fold collar in half to outside.
Press seams.

☐	M
◺	A
◎	B
⊡	C
▽	D
■	E
△	F
⊠	G
⊞	H

SLEEVES

BACK AND FRONT

BOBBLE AND CABLE
SWEATER

PANEL A

1st row P 19(27: 35).
2nd row K2, * [K1, P1, K1] all into next st, K3 tog; rep from * 3(5: 7) times more, K1.
3rd row As 1st row.
4th row K2, * K3 tog, [K1, P1, K1] all into next st; rep from * 3(5: 7) times more, K1.
These 4 rows form the rep of patt.

PANEL B

1st row P 19(27: 35).
2nd row K1, * K3 tog, [K1, P1, K1] all into next st; rep from * 3(5: 7) times more, K2.
3rd row As 1st row.
4th row K1, * [K1, P1, K1] all into next st, K3 tog; rep from * 3(5: 7) times more, K2.
These 4 rows form the rep of patt.

PANEL C

1st row K1 tbl, P2, K5, P2, K1 tbl.
2nd row P1 tbl, K2, P5, K2, P1 tbl.
3rd row K1 tbl, P2, C5K, P2, K1 tbl.
4th row As 2nd row.
5th and 6th rows As 1st and 2nd rows.
7th row K1 tbl, P2, K2, MB, K2, P2, K1 tbl.
8th row As 2nd row.
These 8 rows form the rep of patt.

PANEL D

1st row P6, [P1, K2 tbl] twice, P11, [K2 tbl, P1] twice, P6.
2nd row K6, [K1, P2 tbl] twice, K11, [P2 tbl, K1] twice, K6.
3rd row P7, C5P, P5, MB, P5, C5P, P7.
4th row As 2nd row.
5th row P6, T3B, P1, T3F, P9, T3B, P1, T3F, P6.
6th row K3, [K3, P2 tbl] twice, K9, [P2 tbl, K3] twice, K3.

MATERIALS

17(18: 19) 50 g balls of Hayfield Raw Cotton Classics DK.
1 pair each of 3¼ mm (No. 10/US 3) and 4 mm (No. 8/US 5) knitting needles.
1 cable needle.

MEASUREMENTS

To fit Bust/ Chest	86–91 cm (97–102) (107–112)	34–36 ins (38–40) (42–44)
All round approx.	107 cm (119: 132)	42 ins (47: 52)
Length to shoulder	65 cm	25½ ins
Sleeve seam	46 cm (47: 48)	18 ins (18½: 19)

TENSION

22 sts and 28 rows to 10 cm (4 ins) over st st using 4 mm (No. 8/US 5) needles.

ABBREVIATIONS

T2B–sl next st to cn to back of work, K1 tbl, then P1 from cn; T2F–sl next st to cn to front of work, P1, then K1 tbl from cn; C2–sl next st to cn to front of work, K1 tbl, then K1 tbl from cn; T3B–sl next st to cn to back of work, K2 tbl, then P1 from cn; T3F–sl next 2 sts to cn to front of work, P1, then K2 tbl from cn; C5K–sl next 3 sts to cn to front of work, K2, sl st from cn back on to left-hand needle and K it, then K rem 2 sts from cn; C5P–sl next 3 sts to cn to front of work, K2 tbl, sl st from cn back on to left-hand needle and P it, then K tbl rem 2 sts from cn; MB–[K1, P1, K1, P1] all into next st, [turn, P4, turn, K4] twice, sl 2nd, 3rd and 4th sts over first st and off needle. Also see page 10.

PANEL E

1st row P4, [T2B] twice, P1, [T2F] twice, P4.
2nd row K4, [P1 tbl, K1, P1 tbl, K3] twice, K1.
3rd row P3, [T2B] twice, P3, [T2F] twice, P3.
4th row K2, [K1, P1 tbl] twice, K5, [P1 tbl, K1] twice, K2.
5th row P2, [T2B] twice, P5, [T2F] twice, P2.

7th row P5, T3B, P3, T3F, P7, T3B, P3, T3F, P5.
8th row K5, P2 tbl, K5, P2 tbl, K7, P2 tbl, K5, P2 tbl, K5.
9th row P4, T3B, P5, T3F, P5, T3B, P5, T3F, P4.
10th row K4, P2 tbl, K7, P2 tbl, K5, P2 tbl, K7, P2 tbl, K4.
11th row P3, [T3B, P7, T3F, P3] twice.
12th row K3, [P2 tbl, K9, P2 tbl, K3] twice.
13th row P2, [T3B, P9, T3F, P1] twice, P1.
14th row K2, [P2 tbl, K11, P2 tbl, K1] twice, K1.
15th row P2, K2 tbl, P5, MB, P5, C5P, P5, MB, P5, K2 tbl, P2.
16th row As 14th row.
17th row P2, [T3F, P9, T3B, P1] twice, P1.
18th row K3, [P2 tbl, K9, P2 tbl, K3] twice.
19th row P3, [T3F, P7, T3B, P3] twice.
20th row K4, P2 tbl, K7, P2 tbl, K5, P2 tbl, K7, P2 tbl, K4.
21st row P4, T3F, P5, T3B, P5, T3F, P5, T3B, P4.
22nd row K5, P2 tbl, K5, P2 tbl, K7, P2 tbl, K5, P2 tbl, K5.
23rd row P5, T3F, P3, T3B, P7, T3F, P3, T3B, P5.
24th row K3, [K3, P2 tbl] twice, K9, [P2 tbl, K3] twice, K3.
25th row P6, T3F, P1, T3B, P9, T3F, P1, T3B, P6.
26th row As 2nd row.
The 3rd–26th rows form the rep of patt.

PANEL E

1st row P4, [T2B] twice, P1, [T2F] twice, P4.
2nd row K4, [P1 tbl, K1, P1 tbl, K3] twice, K1.
3rd row P3, [T2B] twice, P3, [T2F] twice, P3.
4th row K2, [K1, P1 tbl] twice, K5, [P1 tbl, K1] twice, K2.
5th row P2, [T2B] twice, P5, [T2F] twice, P2.

6th row K2, P1 tbl, K1, P1 tbl, K7, P1 tbl, K1, P1 tbl, K2.
7th row P2, MB, P1, T2F, P5, T2B, P1, MB, P2.
8th row K5, [P1 tbl, K5] twice.
9th row P5, T2F, P3, T2B, P5.
10th row K6, [P1 tbl, K3] twice, K3.
11th row P6, MB, P3, MB, P6.
12th row K5, [P1 tbl, K1] 4 times, K4.
These 12 rows form the rep of patt.

BACK

With 3¼ mm (No. 10/US 3) needles cast on 134(150: 166) sts.
1st row (RS) [K2 tbl, P2] 4(6: 8) times, K5, [P2, K2 tbl] 5 times, P2, K5, [P2, K2 tbl] 9 times, P2, K5, [P2, K2 tbl] 5 times, P2, K5, [P2, K2 tbl] to end.
2nd and every foll alt row [P2 tbl, K2] 4(6: 8) times, P5, [K2, P2 tbl] 5 times, K2, P5, [K2, P2 tbl] 9 times, K2, P5, [K2, P2 tbl] 5 times, K2, P5, [K2, P2 tbl] to end.
3rd row [K2 tbl, P2, C2F, P2] 2(3: 4) times, C5K, [P2, C2F, P2, K2 tbl] twice, P2, C2F, P2, C5K, [P2, C2F, P2, K2 tbl] 4 times, P2, C2F, P2, C5K, [P2, C2F, P2, K2 tbl] twice, P2, C2F, P2, C5K, [P2, C2F, P2, K2 tbl] to end.
5th row As 1st row.
7th row [K2 tbl, P2, C2F, P2] 2(3: 4) times, K2, MB, K2, [P2, C2F, P2, K2 tbl] twice, P2, C2F, P2, K2, MB, K2, [P2, C2F, P2, K2 tbl] 4 times, P2, C2F, P2, K2, MB, K2, [P2, C2F, P2, K2 tbl] twice, P2, C2F, P2, K2, MB, K2, [P2, C2F, P2, K2 tbl] to end.
8th row As 2nd row.
These 8 rows form the rep of rib patt. Cont until 23 rows in all have been worked.
Inc row Patt 2(10: 18), m1, [patt 2, m1] 5 times, patt 20, m1, patt 28, m1, [patt 7, m1] twice, patt 28, m1, patt 20, m1, [patt 2, m1] 5 times, patt 2(10: 18). 151(167: 183) sts.
Change to 4 mm (No. 8/US 5) needles and cont in patt as folls:
1st row Work 19(27: 35) sts as 1st row of Panel A, work 11 sts as 1st row of Panel C, work 17 sts as 1st row of Panel E, work 11 sts as 1st row of Panel C, work 35 sts as 1st row of Panel D, work 11 sts as 1st row of Panel C, work 17 sts as 1st row of Panel E, work 11 sts as 1st row of Panel C, work 19(27: 35) sts as 1st row of Panel B.
2nd row Work 19(27: 35) sts as 2nd row of Panel B, work 11 sts as 2nd row of Panel C, work 17 sts as 2nd row of

Panel E, work 11 sts as 2nd row of Panel C, work 35 sts as 2nd row of Panel D, work 11 sts as 2nd row of Panel C, work 17 sts as 2nd row of Panel E, work 11 sts as 2nd row of Panel C, work 19(27: 35) sts as 2nd row of Panel A.
This sets position of patt. Keeping Panel sts correct throughout cont until work meas approx. 65 cm (25½ ins) from beg, ending with a 25th patt row of Panel D.

Shape Shoulders
Cast off 49(57: 65) sts at beg of next 2 rows.
Leave rem 53 sts on a holder for neckband.

FRONT

Work as given for Back until front is 9 rows less than Back to shoulders, thus ending with a 16th patt row of Panel D.

Shape Neck
Next row Patt 60(68: 76), turn and leave rem sts on a spare needle.
Keeping patt correct, cast off 3 sts at

beg of next and foll 2 alt rows, then 2 sts at beg of foll alt row. 49(57: 65) sts.
Work 1 row straight.
Cast off.
Return to sts on spare needle; with RS facing sl first 31 sts on to a holder for neckband, rejoin yarn to neck edge, cast off 3 sts and patt to end.
Cont to match first side, reversing shaping.

SLEEVES

With 3¼ mm (No. 10/US 3) needles cast on 68 sts.
1st row (RS) P2, [K2 tbl, P2] twice, K5, [P2, K2 tbl] 9 times, P2, K5, [P2, K2 tbl] twice, P2.
2nd row [K2, P2 tbl] twice, K2, P5, [K2, P2 tbl] 9 times, K2, P5, [K2, P2 tbl] twice, K2.
This sets position of rib patt. Cont to match Back welt until 23 rows in all have been worked.
Inc row Patt 27, m1, [patt 7, m1] twice, patt 27. 71 sts.
Change to 4 mm (No. 8/US 5) needles and cont in patt as folls:
1st row P7 to set sts as 1st row of Panel A, work 11 sts as 1st row of Panel C, work 35 sts as 1st row of Panel D, work 11 sts as 1st row of Panel C, P7 to set sts as 1st row of Panel B.
2nd row K1, K3 tog, [K1, P1, K1] all into next st, K2 to set sts as 2nd row of Panel B, work 11 sts as 2nd row of Panel C, work 35 sts as 2nd row of Panel D, work 11 sts as 2nd row of Panel C, K2, [K1, P1, K1] all into next st, K3 tog, K1 to set sts as 2nd row of Panel A.
This sets position of patt. Keeping Panel sts correct throughout, *at the same time*, inc one st at each end of next and every foll 3rd row, working inc sts into Panels A and B until there are 113(117: 121) sts, then every foll alt row until there are 161 sts.
Cont without shaping until work meas 46(47: 48) cm [18(18½: 19) ins] from beg, ending with a WS row.
Cast off *loosely*.

NECKBAND

Join right shoulder seam.
With 3¼ mm (No. 10/US 3) needles and RS facing, pick up and K 21 sts evenly down left front neck, K front neck sts

from holder thus; [K2 tbl, P2] twice, [K2 tog tbl, K1 tbl, P2 tog, P1] twice, K2 tog tbl, K1 tbl, [P2, K2 tbl] twice, pick up and K 20 sts evenly up right front neck, then K back neck sts from holder thus; P1, K5, [P2, K2 tbl] twice, P1, P2 tog, K1 tbl, K2 tog tbl, P2, K2 tbl, P2, K into front and back of next st, P2, K2 tbl, P2, K2 tog tbl, K1 tbl, P2 tog, P1, [K2 tbl, P2] twice, K5, P1, cast on one st. 118 sts.
Next row K2, P5, [K2, P2 tbl] 9 times, K2, P5, K2, P2 tbl, K2, P5, [K2, P2 tbl] 11 times, K2, P5, K2, P2 tbl, K2.
This sets position of rib patt. Cont to match Back welt until 15 rows in all have been worked.
Cast off *loosely* in patt.

TO MAKE UP

Do not press.
Join left shoulder and neckband seam. Sew in sleeves, with centre of sleeve to shoulder seam. Join side and sleeve seams.
Press seams lightly on WS according to instructions on ball band, omitting ribbing.

SIMPLE CABLE SWEATER

BACK

With 3¾ mm (No. 9/US 4) needles cast on 74(94: 114: 134: 154) sts.
1st row (RS) K2, [P2, K2] to end.
2nd row P2, [K2, P2] to end.
Rep these 2 rows until work meas 5(6: 6: 7: 7) cm [2(2¼: 2¼: 2¾: 2¾) ins] from beg, ending with a WS row.
Inc row Rib 10(8: 7: 7: 8), m1, [rib 1(1: 2: 2: 3), m1, rib 1(2: 2: 3: 3), m1] 27(26: 25: 24: 23) times, rib to end. 129(147: 165: 183: 201) sts.
Change to 4½ mm (No. 7/US 6) needles and cont in patt as folls:
1st row [K1, P1, K1, P6] to last 3 sts, K1, P1, K1.
2nd row [P1, K1, P1, K6] to last 3 sts, P1, K1, P1.
3rd row As 1st row.
4th row [P1, K1, P1, C6] to last 3 sts, P1, K1, P1.
5th–8th rows Rep 1st and 2nd rows twice.
These 8 rows form the rep of patt.
Cont until work meas 42(57: 64: 68: 72) cm [16½(22½: 25¼: 26¾: 28¼) ins] from beg, ending with a WS row.

Shape Shoulders

Keeping patt correct, cast off 22(26: 30: 34: 37) sts at beg of next 2 rows, then 22(26: 29: 33: 37) sts at beg of foll 2 rows.
Leave rem 41(43: 47: 49: 53) sts on a holder for collar.

FRONT

Work as given for Back until front meas 36(50: 56: 60: 64) cm [14¼(19¾: 22: 23½: 25¼) ins] from beg, ending with a WS row.

Shape Neck

Next row Patt 52(60: 68: 76: 84), turn and leave rem sts on a spare needle.
Keeping patt correct, dec one st at neck edge on next 6 rows, then every foll alt row until 44(52: 59: 67: 74) sts rem.
Cont without shaping until work meas same as Back to shoulders, ending with a WS row.

MATERIALS

13(20: 24: 28: 32) 50 g balls of Hayfield Brig Aran Classics.
1 pair each of 3¾ mm (No. 9/US 4) and 4½ mm (No. 7/US 6) knitting needles.
Set of four 3¾ mm (No. 9/US 4) double-pointed needles.
1 cable needle.

MEASUREMENTS

To fit Chest/ Bust	66–71 cm (76–81: 86–91: 97–102: 107–112)	26–28 ins (30–32: 34–36: 38–40: 42–44)
All round approx.	89 cm (99: 109: 122: 134)	34 ins (39: 43: 48: 53)
Length to shoulder	42 cm (57: 64: 68: 72)	16½ ins (22½: 25¼: 26¾: 28¼)
Sleeve seam	28 cm (37: 42: 46: 50)	11 ins (14½: 16½: 18: 19¾)

TENSION

30 sts and 28 rows to 10 cm (4 ins) over patt using 4½ mm (No. 7/US 6) needles.

ABBREVIATIONS

C6–sl next 3 sts to cn to front of work, K3, then K3 from cn. Also see page 10.

Shape Shoulder

Keeping patt correct, cast off 22(26: 30: 34: 37) sts at beg of next row.
Work 1 row straight, then cast off rem 22(26: 29: 33: 37) sts.
Return to sts on spare needle; with RS facing sl first 25(27: 29: 31: 33) sts on to a holder for collar, rejoin yarn to neck edge and patt to end.
Cont to match first side, reversing all shaping.

SLEEVES

With 3¾ mm (No. 9/US 4) needles cast on 38(42: 46: 46: 50) sts and work 5(6: 6: 7: 7) cm [2(2¼: 2¼: 2¾: 2¾) ins] in rib as for Back welt, ending with a WS row.
Inc row Rib 1(9: 9: 4: 4), m1, [rib 2(1: 1: 1: 1), m1] 18(23: 28: 37: 42) times, rib to end. 57(66: 75: 84: 93) sts.
Change to 4½ mm (No. 7/US 6) needles.
Cont in patt as for Back, *at the same time*, inc one st at each end of the 3rd and every foll alt(3rd: 3rd: 3rd: 3rd) row, working inc sts into patt until there are 105(116: 129: 140: 153) sts.
Cont without shaping until work meas 28(37: 42: 46: 50) cm [11(14½: 16½: 18: 19¾) ins] from beg, ending with a WS row.
Cast off *loosely*.

COLLAR

Join shoulder seams.
With set of four 3¾ mm (No. 9/US 4) needles and RS facing, pick up and K 20(22: 23: 23: 24) sts evenly down left front neck, K front neck sts from holder, pick up and K 20(22: 23: 23: 24) sts evenly up right front neck, then K back neck sts from holder dec 2 sts evenly across them. 104(112: 120: 124: 132) sts.
Work 10 cm (4 ins) in rounds of K2, P2 rib.
Cast off *loosely* in rib.

TO MAKE UP

Do not press.
Sew in sleeves, with centre of sleeve to shoulder seam. Join side and sleeve seams. Turn collar in half to outside. Press seams lightly on WS according to instructions on ball band, omitting ribbing.

TWEEDY JACKET WITH EMBROIDERY

BACK

With 3¼ mm (No. 10/US 3) needles and M, cast on 93(99: 105) sts.
1st row (RS) K1, [P1, K1] to end.
2nd row P1, [K1, P1] to end.
Rep these 2 rows twice more inc one st in centre of last row. 94(100: 106) sts.
Change to 4 mm (No. 8/US 5) needles.
Beg with a K row and working in st st throughout, cont in patt from Chart starting and ending rows as indicated, *at the same time*, inc one st at each end of the 10th and every foll 9th row until there are 112(118: 124) sts.
Cont without shaping until 96(98: 100) rows in all have been worked in st st.

Shape Armholes

Cast off 4(5: 6) sts at beg of next 2 rows.
Dec one st at each end of next 4 rows, then every foll alt row until 86(90: 94) sts rem.
Cont without shaping until 154(158: 162) rows in all have been worked in st st.

Shape Shoulders

Cast off 9(10: 11) sts at beg of next 4 rows, then 9 sts at beg of foll 2 rows.
Leave rem 32 sts on a holder.

LEFT FRONT

With 4 mm (No. 8/US 5) needles and M, cast on 3 sts.
Beg with a K row and working in st st throughout, cont as folls:
Work 1 row. **
[Cast on 2 sts at beg of next row and 3 sts at beg of foll row] 4(5: 6) times.
Cast on 2 sts at beg of next row. 25(30: 35) sts.
Next row Cast on 3 sts, K these 3 sts, K 7(12: 17)M, 2C, 16M.
Next row Cast on 2 sts, P these 2 sts, P 16M, 2C, 10(15: 20)M.
Working in M only, cast on 3(3: 2) sts at beg of next row and 2 sts at beg of foll row.
Next row Cast on 3(3: 2) sts, K these 3(3: 2) sts, K 6(11: 15)M, 2C, 27M.

MATERIALS

9(10: 11) 50 g balls of Emu Superwash DK in main colour, M.
1 ball in each of 6 contrast colours, A, B, C, D, E and F.
1 pair each of 3¼ mm (No. 10/US 3) and 4 mm (No. 8/US 5) knitting needles.
3¼ mm (No. 10/US 3) circular needle, 100 cm (42 ins) long.
10 buttons.

MEASUREMENTS

To fit Bust	86 cm	34 ins
	(91: 97)	(36: 38)
All round approx.	102 cm	40 ins
	(107: 112)	(42: 44)
Length to shoulder	53 cm	20¾ ins
	(54: 55)	(21¼: 21¾)
Sleeve seam	40 cm	15¾ ins

TENSION

22 sts and 30 rows to 10 cm (4 ins) over st st using 4 mm (No. 8/US 5) needles.

ABBREVIATIONS

See page 10.

NOTE

When working patts from Chart, read odd rows (K) from right to left and even rows (P) from left to right. Use a separate length of yarn for each section and twist yarns tog where they join on every row to avoid a hole.

Next row Cast on 2 sts, P these 2 sts, P 27M, 2C, 9(14: 17)M.
Working in M only, cast on 4(2: 2) sts at beg of next row and one st at beg of foll row. 45(48: 51) sts.
Cont in patt from Chart starting and ending rows as indicated, *at the same time*, inc one st at side edge on the 10th and every foll 9th row until there are 54(57: 60) sts.

Cont without shaping until 96(98: 100) rows in all have been worked from Chart.

Shape Armhole

Cast off 4(5: 6) sts at beg of next row.
Work 1 row straight.
Dec one st at armhole edge on next 4 rows, then every foll alt row until 41(43: 45) sts rem.
Cont without shaping until 135(139: 143) rows in all have been worked from Chart.

Shape Neck

Cast off 6 sts at beg of next row, then 3 sts at beg of foll alt row.
Dec one st at neck edge on next and every foll alt row until 27(29: 31) sts rem.
Cont without shaping until 154(158: 162) rows in all have been worked from Chart.

Shape Shoulder

Cast off 9(10: 11) sts at beg of next and foll alt row. Work 1 row straight, then cast off rem 9 sts.

RIGHT FRONT

Work as given for Left Front to **.
Cast on 3 sts at beg of next 5 rows.
[Cast on 2 sts at beg of next row and 3 sts at beg of foll row] 0(1: 2) times. 18(23: 28) sts.
Next row Cast on 2 sts, K these 2 sts, K9M, 2C, 7(12: 17)M.
Next row Cast on 3(3: 2) sts, P these 3(3: 2) sts, P 7(12: 17)M, 2C, 11M.
Working in M only, cast on 2 sts at beg of next row and 3(3: 2) sts at beg of foll row.
[Cast on 2 sts at beg of next row and 3(2: 2) sts at beg of foll row] twice.
Cast on 2 sts at beg of next 2 rows.
Next row Cast on one st, K this st, K27M, 2C, 13(16: 19)M.
Next row Cast on 2 sts, P these 2 sts, P 13(16: 19)M, 2C, 28M. 45(48: 51) sts.
Cont in patt from Chart starting and ending rows as indicated, *at the same time*, inc one st at side edge on the 10th

and every foll 9th row until there are 54(57: 60) sts.

Cont without shaping until 97(99: 101) rows in all have been worked from Chart.

Cont to match Left Front, reversing all shaping as set.

LEFT SLEEVE

With 3¼ mm (No. 10/US 3) needles and M, cast on 49(51: 53) sts and work 6 rows in rib as for Back welt, inc 0(2: 4) sts evenly across the last row. 49(53: 57) sts.

Change to 4 mm (No. 8/US 5) needles and cont in patt as folls: **

Next row K 2(4: 6)M, K next 45 sts as row 1 of Chart for 1st size Right Front, K 2(4: 6) M.

Next row P 2(4: 6)M, P next 45 sts as row 2 of Chart for 1st size Right Front, P 2(4: 6) M.

This sets position of patt. Beg with row 3 and working in st st throughout cont in patt from Chart, *at the same time*, inc one st at each end of the 3rd and every foll 4th row, working inc sts into M with "4 st squares" in C at random, until there are 103(107: 111) sts.

Cont without shaping until 114 rows in all have been worked in st st.

Shape Top

Keeping patt correct cast off 4(5: 6) sts at beg of next 2 rows, then 4 sts at beg of next 8 rows.

Dec one st at each end of next and every foll alt row until 47(49: 51) sts rem. Work 1 row straight.

Cast off 2 sts at beg of next 6 rows.

Cast off rem 35(37: 39) sts.

RIGHT SLEEVE

Work as given for Left Sleeve to **.

Next row K 2(4: 6) M, K next 45 sts as row 1 of Chart for 1st size Left Front, K 2(4: 6)M.

Next row P 2(4: 6)M, P next 45 sts as row 2 of Chart for 1st size Left Front, P 2(4: 6)M.

This sets position of patt. Cont to match Left Sleeve.

BUTTONHOLE BAND

Join shoulder seams.

With 3¼ mm (No. 10/US 3) circular needle, M and RS facing, pick up and K 31 (32: 33) sts evenly along cast on sts of right front from side edge to point, one st from point and mark this st, 24(26: 28) sts to front edge, one st from front corner, 118(122: 126) sts up front edge to neck, one st from corner, 31(32: 33) sts up front neck, then K first 16 sts from holder at back neck. 223(231: 239) sts.

Beg with a 2nd row, work 2 rows in rib as for Back welt, *at the same time*, inc one st at each side of marked st on every row. 227(235: 243) sts.

Next row Rib 48(50: 51), [cast off 2 sts, rib 11 including st already on needle after casting off] 10 times, rib 15(20: 26), m1, P1, m1, rib to end.

Next row Rib to end, casting on 2 sts over each 2 cast off, still inc at each side of marked st.

Work 2 more rows in rib as set, still inc as before.

Cast off *loosely* in rib.

BUTTON BAND

With 3¼ mm (No. 10/US 3) circular needle, M and RS facing, K rem 16 sts from holder at back neck, pick up and K 31(32: 33) sts evenly down left front neck, one st from corner, 118(122: 126) sts to lower edge, one st from front corner, 24(26: 28) sts along cast on sts to point, one st from point and mark this st, then 31(32: 33) sts to side edge. 223(231: 239) sts.

Beg with a 2nd row, work 6 rows in rib as for Back welt, *at the same time*, inc one st at each side of marked st on every row.

Cast off *loosely* in rib.

TO MAKE UP

Press work lightly on WS according to instructions on ball band, omitting ribbing.

Using A, D and F, work embroidery to motifs using Chart as a guide:

With F work all stems in Chain st.

Work Trellis st across 3 large flowers knitted in C as folls: lay D across space as required to form a lattice patt, then with A work a small cross st at each intersection. With A, work in Stem st around outer edge of these same flowers, then work looped edge as shown on Chart. Work Trellis st across empty space in centre of 3 large flowers knitted in A as folls: lay D across space as required to form a lattice patt, then with F work a small cross st at each intersection.

Sew in sleeves, gathering tops to fit.

Join side and sleeve seams. Join bands at centre back neck.

Press seams. Sew on buttons.

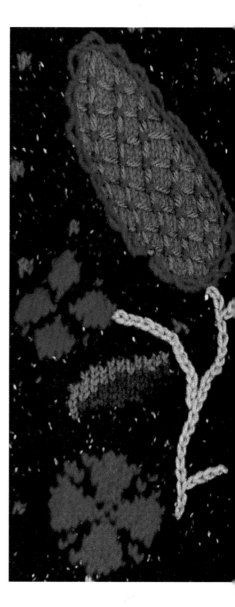

KEY
☐ M	• C	⊘ F chain stitch embroidery
☒ B	⊘ D	∕ stem stitch embroidery in A
⊡ A	◪ E	

BACK AND FRONT

ARAN COAT

MATERIALS

32(33: 34) 50 g balls of Hayfield
Sport Aran
1 pair each of 3¾ mm (No. 9/US 4),
4 mm (No. 8/US 5) and 5 mm
(No. 6/US 7) knitting needles.
1 cable needle.
11 buttons.

MEASUREMENTS

To fit Bust	86 cm	34 ins
	(91: 97)	(36: 38)
Length to	84 cm	33 ins
shoulder	(85: 86)	(33½: 33¾)
Sleeve seam	47 cm	18½ ins

TENSION

25 sts and 24 rows to 10 cm (4 ins)
over patt using 5 mm (No. 6/US 7)
needles.

ABBREVIATIONS

MB–make bobble, [K1, P1, K1] all
into next st, turn, P3, turn, K3,
turn, P3, turn, K3, lift 2nd and 3rd
sts over first st and off needle; C6B–
sl next 3 sts to cn to back of work,
K3, then K3 from cn; C6F–sl next
3 sts to cn to front of work, K3,
then K3 from cn; C4F–sl next 3 sts
to cn to front of work, P1, then K3
from cn; C4B–sl next st to cn to
back of work, K3, then P1 from cn;
T2B–K into front of 2nd st on left-
hand needle, then P into first st
allowing both sts to fall from
needle; T2F–P into front of 2nd st
on left-hand needle, then K into
back of first st allowing both sts to
fall from needle. Also see page 10.

PANEL A

1st row K2, P3, K4, P6, K4, P3, K2.
2nd row P2, K3, P4, C6B, P4, K3, P2.
3rd row As 1st row.
4th row P2, [C4F, P2, C4B] twice, P2.
5th row K3, P3, [K2, P3] 3 times, K3.
6th row P3, [C4F, C4B, P2] twice, P1.
7th row [K4, P6] twice, K4.
8th row P2, MB, P1, C6F, P4, C6B,
P1, MB, P2.
9th row As 7th row.
10th row P3, [C4B, C4F, P2] twice,
P1.
11th row As 5th row.
12th row P2, [C4B, P2, C4F] twice,
P2.
13th row As 1st row.
14th row P2, K3, P4, C6F, P4, K3, P2.
15th row As 1st row.
16th–19th rows As 4th–7th rows.
20th row P2, MB, P1, C6B, P4, C6F,
P1, MB, P2.
21st row As 7th row.
22nd row As 10th row.
23rd row As 5th row.
24th row As 12th row.
These 24 rows form the rep of patt.

PANEL B

1st row K5, P8, K5.
2nd row P4, T2B, K6, T2F, P4.
3rd row K4, P1, K1, P6, K1, P1, K4.
4th row P3, T2B, P1, K6, P1, T2F, P3.
5th row K3, P1, K2, P6, K2, P1, K3.
6th row P2, T2B, P2, C6F, P2, T2F,
P2.
7th row K2, P1, K3, P6, K3, P1, K2.
8th row P1, T2B, P3, K6, P3, T2F, P1.
9th row K1, P1, K4, P6, K4, P1, K1.
10th row P1, T2F, P3, K6, P3, T2B,
P1.
11th row As 7th row.
12th row P2, T2F, P2, C6F, P2, T2B,
P2.
13th row As 5th row.
14th row P3, T2F, P1, K6, P1, T2B,
P3.
15th row As 3rd row.
16th row P4, T2F, K6, T2B, P4.
These 16 rows form the rep of patt.

PANEL C

1st row K7.
2nd row P7.
3rd–6th rows Rep 1st and 2nd rows twice.
7th row K7.
8th row MB, P6.
9th row K7.
10th–19th rows Rep 1st and 2nd rows 5 times.
20th row MB, P6.
21st–24th rows Rep 1st and 2nd rows twice.
These 24 rows form the rep of patt.

BACK

With 4 mm (No. 8/US 5) needles cast on 204(208: 212) sts and work 6 rows in garter st.
Inc row K 11(13: 15), * m1, [K3, m1] 5 times, K41; rep from * twice more, m1, [K3, m1] 5 times, K to end. 228(232: 236) sts.
Change to 5 mm (No. 6/US 7) needles and cont in patt as folls:
1st row (WS) [K1, P1] 4(5: 6) times, K1, [work 24 sts as 1st row of Panel A, K10, work 18 sts as 1st row of Panel B, K10] 3 times, work 24 sts as 1st row of Panel A, K1, [P1, K1] to end.
2nd row [K1, P1] 4(5: 6) times, K1, [work 24 sts as 2nd row of Panel A, P10, work 18 sts as 2nd row of Panel B, P10] 3 times, work 24 sts as 2nd row of Panel A, K1, [P1, K1] to end.
This sets position of patt. Keeping Panel sts correct throughout, end sts in moss st and rem sts in reverse st st, work 7 more rows.

Shape Skirt
10th row Patt 33(35: 37), P2 tog, P8, patt 18, P2 tog, P8, patt 24, P2 tog, P8, patt 18, P8, P2 tog tbl, patt 24, P8, P2 tog tbl, patt 18, P8, P2 tog tbl, patt to end.
Work 9 rows straight.
20th row Patt 33(35: 37), P2 tog, P7, patt 18, P2 tog, P7, patt 24, P2 tog, P7, patt 18, P7, P2 tog tbl, patt 24, P7, P2 tog tbl, patt 18, P7, P2 tog tbl, patt to end.
Work 9 rows straight.
Cont as set, dec 6 sts across next and every foll 10th row until 204 (208: 212) sts rem, then every foll 8th row until 168(172: 176) sts rem, keeping decs in line on reverse st st.
Cont without shaping until work meas 57 cm (22½ ins) from beg, ending with a WS row.

Shape Armholes
Keeping patt correct, cast off 10(11: 12) sts at beg of next 2 rows. 148(150: 152) sts.
Cont without shaping until work meas 81(82: 83) cm [32(32¼: 32¾) ins] from beg, ending with a WS row.

Shape Neck
Next row Patt 49(50: 51), turn and leave rem sts on a spare needle.
Keeping patt correct, cast off 4 sts at beg of next row, then 3 sts at beg of foll 2 alt rows.
Dec one st at neck edge on next 2 rows.
Cast off rem 37(38: 39) sts.
Return to sts on spare needle; with RS facing sl first 50 sts on to a holder for Collar, rejoin yarn to neck edge, cast off 4 sts and patt to end.
Cont to match first side, reversing shaping.

POCKET LININGS (make 2)

With 5 mm (No. 6/US 7) needles cast on 30 sts.
1st row (RS) P6, work 18 sts as 12th row of Panel B, P6.
2nd row K6, work 18 sts as 13th row of Panel B, K6.
This sets position of patt. Keeping Panel sts correct throughout and rem sts in reverse st st, cont until 35 rows in all have been worked, thus ending with a 14th row of Panel B. Leave sts on a holder.

LEFT FRONT

With 4 mm (No. 8/US 5) needles cast on 98(100: 102) sts and work 6 rows in garter st. **
Inc row K 11(13: 15), m1, [K5, m1] 3 times, K43, m1, [K5, m1] 3 times, K to end. 106(108: 110) sts.
Change to 5 mm (No. 6/US 7) needles and cont in patt as folls:
1st row (WS) K11, work 24 sts as 1st row of Panel A, K10, work 18 sts as 1st row of Panel B, K10, work 24 sts as 1st row of Panel A, K1, [P1, K1] to end.
2nd row [K1, P1] 4(5: 6) times, K1, work 24 sts as 2nd row of Panel A, P10, work 18 sts as 2nd row of Panel B, P10, work 24 sts as 2nd row of Panel A, P11.
This sets position of patt. Keeping

Panel sts correct throughout, side sts in moss st and rem sts in reverse st st, work 7 more rows.

Shape Skirt
10th row Patt 33(35: 37), P2 tog, P8, patt 18, P2 tog, P8, patt 24, P2 tog, P9.
Work 9 rows straight.
Cont as set, dec 3 sts across next and every foll 10th row until 94(96: 98) sts rem, then every foll 8th row until 88(90: 92) sts rem, keeping decs in line on reverse st st. Work 6 rows straight.

Place Pocket
Next row Patt 27, sl next 30 sts on to a holder, with WS facing patt to end across sts of first pocket lining, patt to end.
Cont as set dec 3 sts on next and every foll 8th row until 76(78: 80) sts rem.
Cont without shaping until work meas same as Back to armholes, ending with a WS row.

Shape Armhole
Keeping patt correct, cast off 10(11: 12) sts at beg of next row. 66(67: 68) sts.
Cont without shaping until work meas 78(79: 80) cm [30¾(31: 31½) ins] from beg, ending with a RS row.

Shape Neck
Keeping patt correct, cast off 8 sts at beg of next row, 5 sts at beg of foll 2 alt rows, 4 sts at beg of foll alt row, 3 sts at beg of foll alt row, then 2 sts at beg of foll 2 alt rows. 37(38: 39) sts.
Cont without shaping until work meas same as Back to shoulders, ending with a WS row.
Cast off.

RIGHT FRONT

Work as given for Left Front to **.
Inc row K13, m1, [K5, m1] 3 times, K43, m1, [K5, m1] 3 times, K to end. 106(108: 110) sts.
Change to 5 mm (No. 6/US 7) needles and cont in patt as folls:
1st row (WS) [K1, P1] 4(5: 6) times, K1, work 24 sts as 1st row of Panel A, K10, work 18 sts as 1st row of Panel B, K10, work 24 sts as 1st row of Panel A, K11.
2nd row P11, work 24 sts as 2nd row of Panel A, P10, work 18 sts as 2nd row of Panel B, P10, work 24 sts as 2nd row of Panel A, K1, [P1, K1] to end.

This sets position of patt. Keeping Panel sts correct throughout, side sts in moss st and rem sts in reverse st st, work 7 more rows.

Shape Skirt
10th row P9, P2 tog tbl, patt 24, P8, P2 tog tbl, patt 18, P8, P2 tog tbl, patt to end.
Work 9 rows straight.
Cont as set, dec 3 sts across next and every foll 10th row until 94(96: 98) sts rem, then every foll 8th row until 88(90: 92) sts rem, keeping decs in line on reverse st st. Work 6 rows straight.

Place Pocket
Next row Patt 31(33: 35), sl next 30 sts on to a holder, with WS facing, patt to end across sts of 2nd pocket lining, patt to end.
Cont to match Left Front, reversing all shaping and position of patt as set.

SLEEVES

With 4 mm (No. 8/US 5) needles cast on 57(59: 61) sts.
1st row (RS) K1, [P1, K1] to end.
2nd row P1, [K1, P1] to end.
Rep these 2 rows until work meas 10 cm (4 ins) from beg, ending with a WS row.
Inc row Rib 5(7: 9), m1, [rib 1, m1] 46(44: 42) times, rib to end. 104 sts.
Change to 5 mm (No. 6/US 7) needles and cont in patt as folls:
1st row K1, P1, K1, work 7 sts as 1st row of Panel C, work 24 sts as 1st row of Panel A, [work 18 sts as 1st row of Panel B] twice, work 24 sts as 1st row of Panel A, work 7 sts as 1st row of Panel C, K1, P1, K1.
2nd row K1, P1, K1, work 7 sts as 2nd row of Panel C, work 24 sts as 2nd row of Panel A, [work 18 sts as 2nd row of Panel B] twice, work 24 sts as 2nd row of Panel A, work 7 sts as 2nd row of Panel C, K1, P1, K1.
This sets position of patt. Keeping Panel sts correct throughout and end sts in moss st as set, inc one st at each end of the 3rd and every foll 5th row, until there are 130(134: 138) sts.
Cont without shaping until work meas 47 cm (18½ ins) from beg, ending with a WS row. Place a marker at each end of last row.
Work a further 15(16: 17) rows.
Next row Cast off 49(51: 53) sts, [sl st

on right-hand needle back on to left-hand needle and cast off 4 sts tog] 8 times, cast off rem sts.

BUTTONHOLE BAND

With 3¾ mm (No. 9/US 4) needles and RS facing, pick up and K 163(165: 169) sts evenly up right front edge. Beg with a 2nd row, work 3 rows in rib as for Cuffs.
Next row Rib 37(39: 43), [cast off 2 sts, rib 18] 6 times, cast off 2 sts, rib 4.
Next row Rib to end, casting on 2 sts over each 2 cast off.
Work 4 more rows, then cast off *loosely* in rib as set.

BUTTON BAND

Work to match Buttonhole Band, omitting buttonholes.

BELT

With 4 mm (No. 8/US 5) needles cast on 21 sts.
1st row P2, K17, P2.
Rep this row throughout until work meas 50 cm (19¾ ins) from beg.
Cast off.

COLLAR

Join shoulder seams.
With 3¾ mm (No. 9/US 4) needles and RS facing, beg in centre of front band, pick up and K 33 sts evenly up right front neck and 9 sts down right back neck, K back neck sts from holder dec 13 sts evenly across them, then pick up and K9 sts evenly up left back neck and 33 sts down left front neck, ending in centre of front band. 121 sts.
Beg with a 2nd row, work 8 cm (3¼ ins) in rib as for Cuffs.
Cast off in rib.

POCKET TOPS

With 3¾ mm (No. 9/US 4) needles and RS facing, K to end across sts on holder, dec one st in centre. 29 sts.
Work 3 cm (1¼ ins) in rib as for Cuffs.
Cast off *loosely* in rib.

TO MAKE UP

Do not press.
Sew in sleeves, with rows above markers to cast off sts at underarm. Join side and sleeve seams. Sew belt to Back. Sew down pocket tops and pocket linings.
Press seams lightly on WS according to instructions on ball band, omitting ribbing. Sew 7 buttons to front edge and 4 buttons on belt.

LACE AND TEXTURE PANELLED SWEATER

PANEL A

1st row P2, [K1, P1] 3 times. P1.
2nd row K2, [P1, K1] 3 times, K1.
3rd–8th rows Rep 1st and 2nd rows 3 times.
9th row P2, C5, P2.
10th row As 2nd row.
11th–16th rows Rep 1st and 2nd rows 3 times.
These 16 rows form the rep of patt.

PANEL B

1st row K6, K2 tog, yfwd, K1, yfwd, sl 1, K1, psso, K6.
2nd row P7, K1, P1, K1, P7.
3rd row K5, K2 tog, yrn, P1, K1, P1, yon, sl 1, K1, psso, K5.
4th row As 2nd row.
5th row K4, K2 tog, yfwd, [K1, P1] twice, K1, yfwd, sl 1, K1, psso, K4.
6th row P5, [K1, P1] 4 times, P4.
7th row K3, K2 tog, yrn, [P1, K1] 3 times, P1, yon, sl 1, K1, psso, K3.
8th row As 6th row.
9th row K2, K2 tog, yfwd, [K1, P1] 4 times, K1, yfwd, sl 1, K1, psso, K2.
10th row P3, [K1, P1] 6 times, P2.
11th row K1, K2 tog, yrn, [P1, K1] 5 times, P1, yon, sl 1, K1, psso, K1.
12th row As 10th row.
13th row K1, yfwd, sl 1, K1, psso, [P1, K1] 5 times, P1, K2 tog, yfwd, K1.
14th row As 10th row.
15th row K2, yfwd, sl 1, K1, psso, [K1, P1] 4 times, K1, K2 tog, yfwd, K2.
16th row As 6th row.
17th row K3, yfwd, sl 1, K1, psso, [P1, K1] 3 times, P1, K2 tog, yfwd, K3.
18th row As 6th row.
19th row K4, yfwd, sl 1, K1, psso, [K1, P1] twice, K1, K2 tog, yfwd, K4.
20th row As 2nd row.
21st row K5, yfwd, sl 1, K1, psso, P1, K1, P1, K2 tog, yfwd, K5.
22nd row As 2nd row.
23rd row K6, yfwd, sl 1, K1, psso, K1, K2 tog, yfwd, K6.
24th row P8, K1, P8.
These 24 rows form the rep of patt.

MATERIALS

13(14: 14) 50 g balls of Hayfield Raw Cotton Classics DK.
1 pair each of 3 mm (No. 11/US 2), 3¼ mm (No. 10/US 3) and 4 mm (No. 8/US 5) knitting needles.
1 cable needle.

MEASUREMENTS

To fit Bust	86 cm (91: 97)	34 ins (36: 38)
All round approx.	102 cm (107: 112)	40 ins (42: 44)
Length to shoulder	59 cm	23¼ ins
Sleeve length	43 cm	17 ins

TENSION

22 sts and 28 rows to 10 cm (4 ins) over st st using 4 mm (No. 8/US 5) needles.

ABBREVIATIONS

C5–sl next 2 sts to cn to back of work, K1, P1, K1, then P1, K1 from cn; T2L–sl next st to cn to front of work, P1, then K1 tbl from cn; T2R–sl next st to cn to back of work, K1 tbl, then P1 from cn; yon–yarn over needle. Also see page 10.

PANEL C

1st row P2, K4, P1, K4, P2.
2nd row K2, P3, K3, P3, K2.
3rd row P2, K2, P5, K2, P2.
4th row K2, P1, K7, P1, K2.
5th row As 3rd row.
6th row As 2nd row.
7th row As 1st row.
8th row K2, P9, K2.
These 8 rows form the rep of patt.

PANEL D

1st row P1, yon, K2, P3, P3 tog, P3, K2, yfwd, K1, yfwd, K2, P3, P3 tog, P3, K2, yrn, P1.
2nd row K2, P2, K7, P7, K7, P2, K2.
3rd row P2, yon, K2, P2, P3 tog, P2, K2, yfwd, K3, yfwd, K2, P2, P3 tog, P2, K2, yrn, P2.
4th row K3, P2, K5, P9, K5, P2, K3.
5th row P3, yon, K2, P1, P3 tog, P1, K2, yfwd, K5, yfwd, K2, P1, P3 tog, P1, K2, yrn, P3.
6th row K4, P2, K3, P11, K3, P2, K4.
7th row P4, yon, K2, P3 tog, K2, yfwd, K7, yfwd, K2, P3 tog, K2, yrn, P4.
8th row K5, P2, K1, P13, K1, P2, K5.
9th row P2 tog, P3, K2, yfwd, K1, yfwd, K2, P3, P3 tog, P3, K2, yfwd, K1, yfwd, K2, P3, P2 tog.
10th row K4, P7, K7, P7, K4.
11th row P2 tog, P2, K2, yfwd, K3, yfwd, K2, P2, P3 tog, P2, K2, yfwd, K3, yfwd, K2, P2, P2 tog.
12th row K3, P9, K5, P9, K3.
13th row P2 tog, P1, K2, yfwd, K5, yfwd, K2, P1, P3 tog, P1, K2, yfwd, K5, yfwd, K2, P1, P2 tog.
14th row K2, P11, K3, P11, K2.
15th row P2 tog, K2, yfwd, K7, yfwd, K2, P3 tog, K2, yfwd, K7, yfwd, K2, P2 tog.
16th row [K1, P13] twice, K1.
These 16 rows form the rep of patt.

PANEL E

1st row P4, [K1 tbl] 3 times, P4.
2nd row K4, [P1 tbl] 3 times, K4.
3rd row P3, T2R, K1 tbl, T2L, P3.
4th row K3, [P1 tbl, K1] 3 times, K2.
5th row P2, T2R, P1, K1 tbl, P1, T2L, P2.
6th row K2, [P1 tbl, K2] 3 times.
7th row P1, T2R, P1, [K1 tbl] 3 times, P1, T2L, P1.
8th row K1, P1 tbl, K2, [P1 tbl] 3 times, K2, P1 tbl, K1.
These 8 rows form the rep of patt.

BACK

With 3 mm (No. 11/US 2) needles cast on 113(117: 121) sts.
1st row (RS) P 0(1: 3), K 2(3: 3), [work 11 sts as 1st row of Panel E, K3] 7 times, work 11 sts as 1st row of Panel E, K 2(3: 3), P 0(1: 3).
2nd row K 0(1: 3), P 2(3: 3), [work 11 sts as 2nd row of Panel E, P3] 7 times, work 11 sts as 2nd row of Panel E, P 2(3: 3), K 0(1: 3).
This sets position of patt. Keeping Panel sts correct throughout and rem sts as set, cont until 31 rows in all have been worked.
P 4 rows.
Inc row P 3(7: 1), [m1, P 6(5: 5), m1, P5] 10(11: 12) times. 133(139: 145) sts.
Change to 4 mm (No. 8/US 5) needles and cont in patt as folls:
1st row K 4(7: 10), work 9 sts as 1st row of Panel A, work 13 sts as 1st row of Panel C, work 17 sts as 1st row of Panel B, work 9 sts as 1st row of Panel A, work 29 sts as 1st row of Panel D, work 9 sts as 1st row of Panel A, work 17 sts as 1st row of Panel B, work 13 sts as 1st row of Panel C, work 9 sts as 1st row of Panel A, K to end.
2nd row P 4(7: 10), work 9 sts as 2nd row of Panel A, work 13 sts as 2nd row of Panel C, work 17 sts as 2nd row of Panel B, work 9 sts as 2nd row of Panel A, work 29 sts as 2nd row of Panel D, work 9 sts as 2nd row of Panel A, work 17 sts as 2nd row of Panel B, work 13 sts as 2nd row of Panel C, work 9 sts as 2nd row of Panel A, P to end.
This sets position of patt. Keeping Panel sts correct throughout work end sts as folls:
3rd row K 4(7: 10), patt to last 4(7: 10) sts, K to end.
4th row P 4(7: 10), patt to last 4(7: 10) sts, P to end.
5th row P 4(7: 10), patt to last 4(7: 10) sts, P to end.
6th row P 4(7: 10), patt to last 4(7: 10) sts, P to end.
7th row P 4(7: 10), patt to last 4(7: 10) sts, P to end.
8th row P 4(7: 10), patt to last 4(7: 10) sts, P to end.
These 8 rows form the rep of Ladder patt at each end. Keeping Panel sts correct and end sts as set, cont until work meas 33 cm (13 ins) from beg, ending with a WS row.

Shape Armholes

Keeping patt correct cast off 5(7: 9) sts at beg of next 2 rows. 123(125: 127) sts.
Cont without shaping until 172 rows in all have been worked from beg, thus ending with an 8th patt row of Panel D.

Shape Neck

Next row Patt 47(48: 49), turn and leave rem sts on a spare needle.
Keeping patt correct, cast off 2 sts at beg of next and foll 3 alt rows.
Cast off rem 39(40: 41) sts.
Return to sts on spare needle; with RS facing sl first 29 sts on to a holder for collar, rejoin yarn to neck edge, cast off 2 sts and patt to end.
Cont to match first side, reversing shaping.

FRONT

Work as given for Back until 164 rows in all have been worked from beg, thus ending with a 16th patt row of Panel D.

Shape Neck

Next row Patt 47(48: 49), turn and leave rem sts on a spare needle.
Keeping patt correct, dec one st at neck edge on next 6 rows, then every foll alt row until 39(40: 41) sts rem.
Cont without shaping until work meas same as Back to shoulders, ending with a WS row.
Cast off.
Return to sts on spare needle; with RS facing sl first 29 sts on to a holder for collar, rejoin yarn to neck edge and patt to end.
Cont to match first side, reversing shaping.

SLEEVES

With 3 mm (No. 11/US 2) needles cast on 57 sts.
1st row (RS) K2, [work 11 sts as 1st row of Panel E, K3] 3 times, work 11 sts as 1st row of Panel E, K2.
2nd row P2, [work 11 sts as 2nd row of Panel E, P3] 3 times, work 11 sts as 2nd row of Panel E, P2.
This sets position of patt. Keeping Panel sts correct throughout and rem sts as set, cont until 31 rows in all have been worked.

P 4 rows.
Inc row P to end inc 6 sts evenly across row. 63 sts.
Change to 4 mm (No. 8/US 5) needles and cont in patt as folls:
1st row K8, work 9 sts as 1st row of Panel A, work 29 sts as 1st row of Panel D, work 9 sts as 1st row of Panel A, K8.
2nd row P8, work 9 sts as 2nd row of Panel A, work 29 sts as 2nd row of Panel D, work 9 sts as 2nd row of Panel A, P8.
This sets position of patt. Keeping Panel sts correct throughout and end sts as set, *at the same time*, inc one st at each end of next and every foll 3rd row, working inc sts into Ladder patt as on Back until there are 111 sts.
Cont without shaping until 132 rows in all have been worked from beg, thus ending with a 16th patt row of Panel D.
Cast off *loosely*.

COLLAR

Join right shoulder seam.
With 3¼ mm (No. 10/US 3) needles and RS facing, pick up and K 20 sts evenly down left front neck, K front neck sts from holder, pick up and K 19 sts evenly up right front neck and 8 sts down right back neck, K back neck sts from holder, then pick up and K 8 sts evenly up left back neck. 113 sts.
1st row K to end.
2nd row P2, [work 11 sts as 2nd row of Panel E, P3] 7 times, work 11 sts as 2nd row of Panel E, P2.
3rd row K2, [work 11 sts as 3rd row of Panel E, K3] 7 times, work 11 sts as 3rd row of Panel E, K2.
This sets position of patt. Keeping Panel sts correct throughout and rem sts as set, cont until 55 rows in all have been worked.
Cast off *loosely* in patt.

TO MAKE UP

Do not press.
Join left shoulder and collar seam, reversing seam on collar to allow for turning. Sew in sleeves, with centre of sleeve to shoulder seam. Join side and sleeve seams. Fold collar in half to outside.
Press seams lightly on WS according to instructions on ball band.

REINDEER, HEART AND SNOWFLAKE
SWEATER AND CARDIGAN

SWEATER

BACK

With 5 mm (No. 6/US 7) needles and M, cast on 126 sts.

1st row (RS) [P2M, take M to WS, K2C, take M to RS] to last 2 sts, P2M.

2nd row [K2M, take M to WS, P2C, take M to RS] to last 2 sts, K2M.

Rep these 2 rows until work meas 5 cm (2 ins) from beg, ending with a WS row and inc 3 sts evenly across the last row. 129 sts.

Change to 6 mm (No. 4/US 9) needles. Beg with a K row and working in st st throughout, cont in patt from Chart starting and ending rows as indicated until 76 rows in all have been worked in st st.

Change to 5½ mm (No. 5/US 8) needles. Cont in patt from Chart as set until 106 rows in all have been worked in st st.

Change to 6 mm (No. 4/US 9) needles. Cont in patt from Chart as set until 122 rows in all have been worked in st st.

Shape Shoulders
Cast off 23 sts at beg of next 4 rows. Leave rem 37 sts on a holder.

FRONT

Work as given for Back until 111 rows in all have been worked in st st.

Shape Neck
Next row Patt 53, turn and leave rem sts on a spare needle.

Keeping patt correct, dec one st at neck edge on next 7 rows. 46 sts. Cont without shaping until 123 rows in all have been worked in st st.

Shape Shoulder
Cast off 23 sts at beg of next row. Work 1 row straight, then cast off rem 23 sts.

Return to sts on spare needle; with WS

MATERIALS

SWEATER: 18 × 50 g balls of Hayfield Sport Chunky in main colour, M.
11 balls in contrast colour, C.
CARDIGAN: 17 balls in main colour, M.
11 balls in contrast colour, C.
1 pair each of 5 mm (No. 6/US 7), 5½ mm (No. 5/US 8) and 6 mm (No. 4/US 9) knitting needles.
Set of four 5 mm (No. 6/US 7) double-pointed needles for Sweater.
5 mm (No. 6/US 7) circular needle 80 cm (30 ins) long and 6 buttons for Cardigan.

MEASUREMENTS

To fit up to Chest	112 cm	44 ins
All round approx.	134 cm	53 ins
Length to shoulder	73 cm	28¾ ins
Sleeve seam	43 cm	17 ins

TENSION

19 sts and 18 rows to 10 cm (4 ins) over Fair Isle patt using 6 mm (No. 4/US 9) needles.

ABBREVIATIONS

See page 10.

NOTE

When working patt from Chart read odd rows (K) from right to left and even rows (P) from left to right. When working motifs use a separate length of yarn for each section and twist yarns tog where they join on every row to avoid a hole. When working Fair Isle strand yarn not in use *loosely* across WS of work to keep fabric elastic.

facing sl first 23 sts on to a holder for neckband, rejoin yarns to neck edge and patt to end.
Cont to match first side, reversing all shaping.

SLEEVES

With 5 mm (No. 6/US 7) needles and M, cast on 30 sts and work 5 cm (2 ins) in striped rib as for Back welt, ending with a RS row.

Inc row Rib 2, [m1, rib 2, m1, rib 1, m1, rib 1] 7 times. 51 sts.

Change to 6 mm (No. 4/US 9) needles. Beg with a K row and working in st st throughout, cont in patt from Chart starting and ending rows as indicated, *at the same time*, inc one st at each end of the 3rd and every foll alt row, working inc sts into patt until there are 107 sts.

Cont without shaping until 68 rows in all have been worked in st st.
Cast off *loosely*.

NECKBAND

Join shoulder seams.
With set of four 5 mm (No. 6/US 7) needles, M and RS facing, K back neck sts from holder, pick up and K 12 sts evenly down left front neck, K front neck sts from holder, then pick up and K 12 sts evenly up right front neck. 84 sts.
Work 5 cm (2 ins) in rounds of K2C, P2M to match Back welt.
Cast off *loosely* in rib using M.

TO MAKE UP

Press work lightly on WS according to instructions on ball band, omitting ribbing.
Sew in sleeves, with centre of sleeve to shoulder seam. Join side and sleeve seams.
Press seams.

BACK, FRONT AND SLEEVES

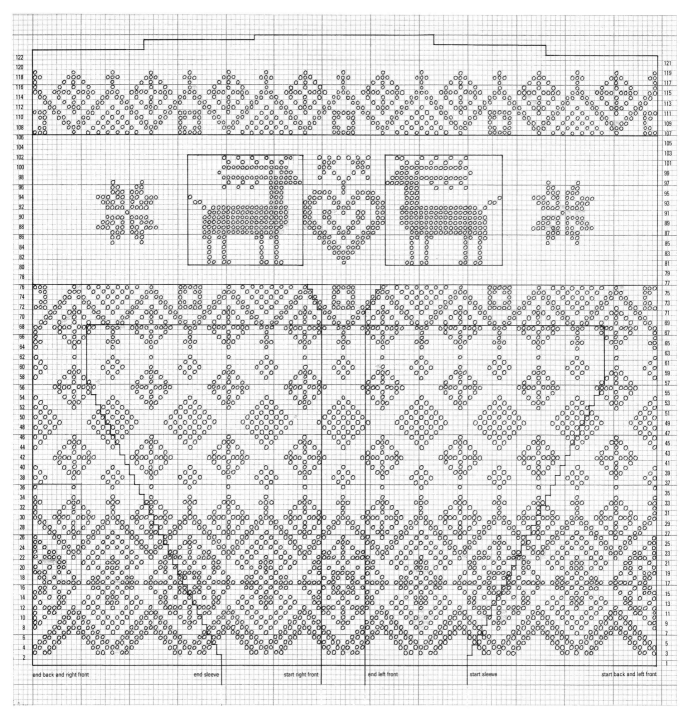

KEY

 M

O C

CARDIGAN

BACK

Work as given for Back of Sweater.

LEFT FRONT

With 5 mm (No. 6/US 7) needles and M, cast on 58 sts and work 5 cm (2 ins) in striped rib as for Back welt of Sweater, ending with a WS row and inc 2 sts evenly across the last row. 60 sts.
Change to 6 mm (No. 4/US 9) needles. Beg with a K row and working in st st throughout, cont in patt from Chart starting and ending rows as indicated until 71 rows in all have been worked in st st.

Shape Front Edge

Keeping patt correct, dec one st at beg of next and every foll alt row until 57 sts rem.
Change to 5½ mm (No. 5/US 8) needles. Using M only work 4 rows, dec one st at neck edge on the 3rd of these rows. 56 sts.
Next row K21M, 2C, 1M, 2C, 6M, 2C, 1M, 2C, 19M.
Next row P2 togM, P18M, 1C, 2M, 1C, 7M, 1C, 2M, 1C, 21M.
This sets position of Reindeer Motif. Cont in patt omitting "Snowflake", dec one st at neck edge on every 3rd row as set until 52 sts rem, then every foll 4th row until 106 rows in all have been worked in st st.
Change to 6 mm (No. 4/US 9) needles. Cont in patt from Chart, still dec at neck edge on every 4th row as set until 46 sts rem.
Cont without shaping until 122 rows in all have been worked in st st.

Shape Shoulder

Cast off 23 sts at beg of next row.
Work 1 row straight, then cast off rem 23 sts.

RIGHT FRONT

Work to match Left Front, reversing position of patt, Reindeer Motif and all shaping.

SLEEVES

Work as given for Sleeves of Sweater.

BUTTONHOLE BAND
(for WOMAN)

Join shoulder seams.
With 5 mm (No. 6/US 7) circular needle and RS facing, pick up and K 76 sts evenly up right front edge to beg of shaping and 52 sts to shoulder, then K first 18 sts from holder at back neck. 146 sts.
Turn and cont in *rows*:
Beg with a 2nd row, work 4 rows in striped rib as for Back welt of Sweater.
Next row Rib 72, [cast off 2 sts, rib 12] 5 times, cast off 2 sts, rib 2.
Next row Rib to end, casting on 2 sts over each 2 cast off.
Work 4 more rows, then cast off in rib using M.

BUTTON BAND

With 5 mm (No. 6/US 7) circular needle, M and RS facing, K rem 19 sts from holder at back neck dec one st in centre, pick up and K 52 sts evenly down left front edge to beg of shaping and 76 sts to lower edge. 146 sts.
Cont to match Buttonhole Band, omitting buttonholes.

BUTTON BAND (for MAN)

Join shoulder seams.
With 5 mm (No. 6/US 7) circular needle, M and RS facing, pick up and K 76 sts evenly up right front edge to beg of shaping and 52 sts to shoulder, then K first 18 sts from holder at back neck. 146 sts.
Turn and cont in *rows*:
Beg with a 2nd row, work 10 rows in striped rib as for Back welt of Sweater.
Cast off in rib using M.

BUTTONHOLE BAND

With 5 mm (No. 6/US 7) circular needle, M and RS facing, K rem 19 sts from holder at back neck dec one st in centre, pick up and K 52 sts evenly down left front edge to beg of shaping and 76 sts to lower edge. 146 sts.
Turn and cont in *rows*:
Beg with a 2nd row, work 4 rows in rib as for Back welt of Sweater.
Next row Rib 2, [cast off 2 sts, rib 12] 5 times, cast off 2 sts, rib 72.
Next row Rib to end, casting on 2 sts over each 2 cast off.
Work 4 more rows, then cast off in rib using M.

TO MAKE UP

Press work lightly on WS according to instructions on ball band, omitting ribbing.
Sew in sleeves, with centre of sleeve to shoulder seam. Join side and sleeve seams. Join ends of bands at centre back neck.
Press seams. Sew on buttons.

CLASSIC FAIR ISLE
FAMILY SWEATERS

MATERIALS

2(3: 3: 4: 4: 5: 5: 6: 6: 7: 7: 8) 50 g balls of Rowan Cabled Mercerised Cotton in main colour, M.
1(1: 2: 2: 2: 2: 2: 3: 3: 3: 4: 4) balls in first contrast colour, A.
1(1: 2: 2: 2: 2: 2: 3: 3: 3: 3: 4) balls in second contrast colour, B.
1(1: 1: 1: 1: 1: 1: 2: 2: 2: 2: 2) balls in third contrast colour, C.
1 ball in 4th contrast colour, D.
1 pair each of 2¾ mm (No. 12/US 1) and 3¼ mm (No. 10/US 3) knitting needles.

MEASUREMENTS

To fit Bust/ Chest	56 cm (61: 66: 71: 76: 81: 86: 91: 97: 102: 107: 112)	22 ins (24: 26: 28: 30: 32: 34: 36: 38: 40: 42: 44)
Actual measurement	61 cm (66: 71: 76: 84: 91: 99: 107: 112: 117: 122: 127)	24 ins (26: 28: 30: 33: 36: 39: 42: 44: 46: 48: 50)
Length to shoulder	36 cm (40: 44: 48: 52: 55: 58: 60: 62: 64: 66: 68)	14¼ ins (15¾: 17¼: 19: 20½: 21¾: 22¾: 23½: 24½: 25¼: 26: 26¾)
Sleeve seam	24 cm (28: 32: 36: 40: 43: 45: 46: 47: 48: 49: 50)	9½ ins (11: 12½: 14¼: 15¾: 17: 17¾: 18: 18½: 19: 19¼: 19¾)

TENSION

32 sts and 32 rows to 10 cm (4 ins) over patt using 3¼ mm (No. 10/ US 3) needles.

ABBREVIATIONS

See page 10.

NOTE

When working patt from Chart, read odd rows (K) from right to left and even rows (P) from left to right. Strand yarn not in use *loosely* across WS of work to keep fabric elastic.

BACK

With 2¾ mm (No. 12/US 1) needles and M, cast on 81(87: 93: 99: 107: 113: 119: 125: 131: 137: 143: 149) sts.
1st row (RS) K1, [P1, K1] to end.
2nd row P1, [K1, P1] to end.
Rep these 2 rows 10(10: 11: 11: 12: 12: 13: 13: 14: 14: 15: 15) times more, then the 1st row again.
Inc row Rib 7(5: 2: 8: 2: 10: 4: 6: 7: 7: 8: 8), [m1, rib 5(5: 5: 4: 4: 3: 3: 2: 2: 2: 2: 2), m1, rib 4(4: 4: 4: 3: 3: 3: 3: 3: 3: 3: 3)] 8(9: 10: 11: 13: 16: 19: 23: 24: 25: 26: 27) times, rib to end. 97(105: 113: 121: 133: 145: 157: 171: 179: 187: 195: 203) sts.

Change to 3¼ mm (No. 10/US 3) needles.
Beg with a K row and working in st st throughout, cont in patt from Chart starting and ending rows as indicated until work meas 36(40: 44: 48: 52: 55: 58: 60: 62: 64: 66: 68) cm [14¼(15¾: 17¼: 19: 20½: 21¾: 22¾: 23½: 24½: 25¼: 26: 26¾) ins] from beg, ending with a P row.

Shape Shoulders

Keeping patt correct, cast off 15(16: 18: 19: 22: 24: 27: 30: 31: 33: 34: 36) sts at beg of next 2 rows, then 14(16: 17: 19: 21: 24: 26: 29: 31: 32: 34: 35) sts at beg of foll 2 rows.
Leave rem 39(41: 43: 45: 47: 49: 51: 53: 55: 57: 59: 61) sts on a holder for neckband.

FRONT

Work as given for Back until front meas 31(35: 39: 42: 46: 49: 51: 53: 55: 56: 58: 60) cm [12¼(13¾: 15¼: 16½: 18: 19¼: 20: 20¾: 21¾: 22: 22¾: 23½) ins] from beg, ending with a P row.

Shape Neck

Next row Patt 40(43: 46: 50: 55: 60: 66: 72: 75: 79: 82: 85), turn and leave rem sts on a spare needle.
Keeping patt correct, dec one st at neck edge on next 9(9: 9: 10: 10: 10: 11: 11: 11: 12: 12: 12) rows, then every foll alt row until 29(32: 35: 38: 43: 48: 53: 59: 62: 65: 68: 71) sts rem.
Cont without shaping until work meas same as Back to shoulders, ending with a P row.

Shape Shoulder

Keeping patt correct, cast off 15(16: 18: 19: 22: 24: 27: 30: 31: 33: 34: 36) sts at beg of next row. Work 1 row straight, then cast off rem 14(16: 17: 19: 21: 24: 26: 29: 31: 32: 34: 35) sts.
Return to sts on spare needle; with RS facing sl first 17(19: 21: 21: 23: 25: 25: 27: 29: 29: 31: 33) sts on to a holder for neckband, rejoin yarns to neck edge and patt to end.
Cont to match first side, reversing all shaping.

SLEEVES

With 2¾ mm (No. 12/US 1) needles and M, cast on 51(53: 55: 57: 61: 63: 65: 67: 69: 71: 73: 75) sts and work 23(23: 25: 25: 27: 27: 29: 29: 31: 31: 33: 33) rows in rib as for Back welt.
Inc row Rib 5(4: 5: 2: 7: 5: 7: 7: 6: 5: 4: 2), [m1, rib 5(4: 3: 3: 3: 3: 2: 2: 2: 2: 2: 2), m1, rib 4(4: 3: 3: 2: 2: 2: 2: 2: 2: 2: 2)] 5(6: 8: 9: 10: 11: 13: 14: 15: 16: 17:

18) times, rib to end. 61(65: 71: 75: 81: 85: 91: 95: 99: 103: 107: 111) sts.
Change to 3¼ mm (No. 10/US 3) needles.
Beg with a K row and working in st st throughout, cont in patt from Chart starting and ending rows as indicated, *at the same time*, inc one st at each end of the 5th and every foll 3rd(3rd: 4th: 4th: 4th: 5th: 5th: 5th: 4th: 4th: 4th: 4th) row, working inc sts into patt until there are 93(99: 107: 113: 121: 127: 135: 141: 149: 155: 163: 169) sts.
Cont without shaping until work meas 24(28: 32: 36: 40: 43: 45: 46: 47: 48: 49: 50) cm [9½(11: 12½: 14¼: 15¾: 17: 17¾: 18: 18½: 19: 19¼: 19¾) ins] from beg, ending with a P row.
Cast off *loosely*.

NECKBAND

Join right shoulder seam.
With 2¾ mm (No. 12/US 1) needles, M and RS facing, pick up and K 19(19: 19: 22: 22: 22: 25: 25: 25: 28: 28: 28) sts evenly down left front neck, K front neck sts from holder, pick up and K 18(18: 18: 21: 21: 21: 24: 24: 24: 27: 27: 27) sts evenly up right front neck, then K back neck sts from holder. 93(97: 101: 109: 113: 117: 125: 129: 133: 141: 145: 149) sts.
Beg with a 2nd row, work 8(8: 8: 8: 9: 9: 9: 9: 10: 10: 10: 10) rows in rib as for Back welt.
Cast off *loosely* in rib.

TO MAKE UP

Press work lightly on WS according to instructions on ball band, omitting ribbing.
Join left shoulder and neckband seam. Sew in sleeves, with centre of sleeve to shoulder seam. Join side and sleeve seams. Press seams.

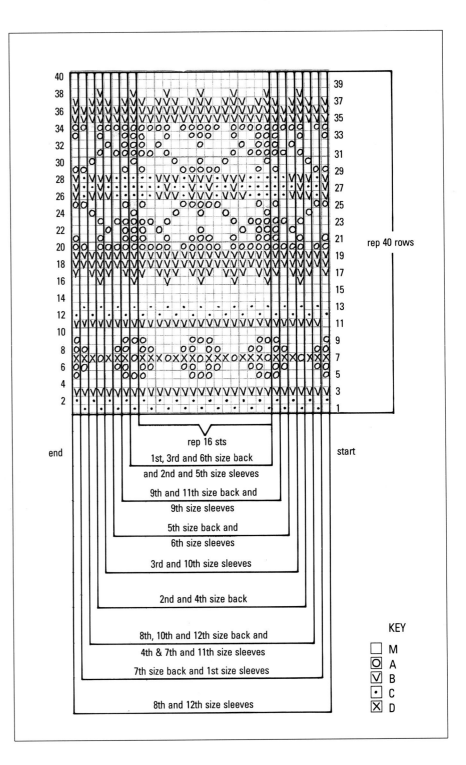

rep 40 rows

end   start

rep 16 sts

1st, 3rd and 6th size back
and 2nd and 5th size sleeves

9th and 11th size back and
9th size sleeves

5th size back and
6th size sleeves

3rd and 10th size sleeves

2nd and 4th size back

8th, 10th and 12th size back and
4th & 7th and 11th size sleeves

7th size back and 1st size sleeves

8th and 12th size sleeves

KEY
☐ M
Ⓞ A
Ⓥ B
· C
Ⓧ D

CLASSIC FAIR ISLE
TAM 'O' SHANTER

CHART 2 ADULTS

MATERIALS

1(2) 50 g balls of Rowan Cabled Mercerised Cotton in main colour, M.
1 ball in each of 4 contrast colours (see Charts).
Set of four $2\frac{3}{4}$ mm (No. 12/US 1) and $3\frac{1}{4}$ mm (No. 10/US 3) double-pointed needles.

MEASUREMENTS

To fit   child
            (women)
Diameter   25 cm $9\frac{3}{4}$ ins
            (29)   ($11\frac{1}{2}$)

TENSION

32 sts and 32 rows to 10 cm (4 ins) over patt using $3\frac{1}{4}$ mm (No. 10/US 3) needles.

ABBREVIATIONS

See page 10.

NOTE

When working patt from Charts, read all rows (K) from right to left. Strand yarn not in use *loosely* across WS of work to keep fabric elastic. When working all inc and dec sts use appropriate yarn so as to keep the flow of patt correct.

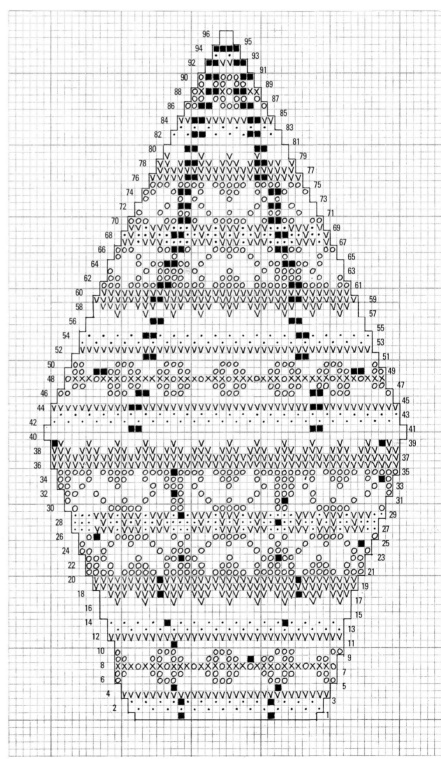

KEY

☐	M
V	A
O	B
·	C
X	D
■	inc 1
■■	k2 tog

BEG WITH BRIM

With 2¾ mm (No. 12/US 1) needles and
M, cast on 120(130) sts.
Work 8(10) rounds in K1, P1 rib.
Change to 3¼ mm (No. 10/US 3)
needles.
Working in st st throughout (every

round K) cont in patt from Chart 1(2),
rep these sts 5 times across every
round knitting into front and back of
all inc sts and K2 tog where shown
until the 82(96) rows are complete.
10 sts.

CHART 1   CHILDS

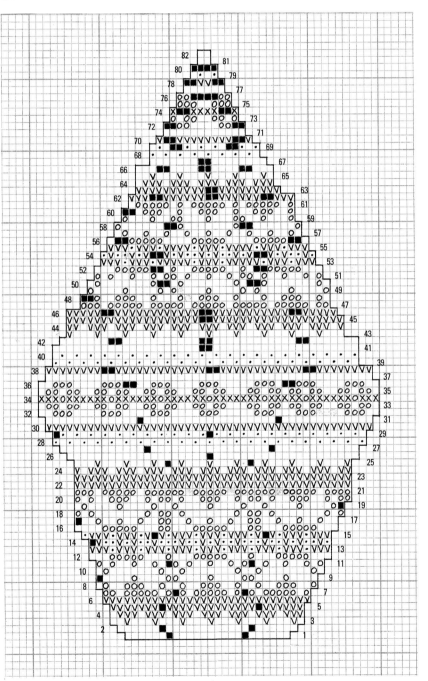

TO MAKE UP

Press work lightly on WS according to
instructions on ball band, omitting
ribbing.
Break off yarn, thread through sts, pull
tight and fasten off.

KEY

☐	M
V	A
O	B
·	C
X	D
■	inc 1
■■	k2 tog

TYROLEAN JACKET

PANEL A

1st row K10, P4, K10.
2nd row P10, K4, P10.
3rd and 4th rows As 1st and 2nd rows.
5th row As 1st row.
6th row P8, C4B, C4F, P8.
7th row K8, P8, K8.
8th row P6, C4BP, C4F, C4FP, P6.
9th row K6, P2, K2, P4, K2, P2, K6.
10th row P4, C4BP, P2, K4, P2, C4FP, P4.
11th row [K4, P2] twice, [P2, K4] twice.
12th row P3, T3B, P4, C4F, P4, T3F, P3.
13th row K3, P2, K5, P4, K5, P2, K3.
14th row P2, T3B, P3, C4B, C4F, P3, T3F, P2.
15th row K2, P2, K4, P8, K4, P2, K2.
16th row P1, T3B, P2, C4BP, K4, C4FP, P2, T3F, P1.
17th row K1, P2, K3, P2, K2, P4, K2, P2, K3, P2, K1.
18th row T3B, P1, C4BP, P2, C4B, P2, C4FP, P1, T3F.
19th row P2, K2, P2, K4, P4, K4, P2, K2, P2.
20th row K2, P2, K2, P4, K4, P4, K2, P2, K2.
21st row As 19th row.
22nd row T3F, P1, C4FP, P2, C4B, P2, C4BP, P1, T3B.
23rd row As 17th row.
24th row P1, T3F, P2, C4FP, K4, C4BP, P2, T3B, P1.
25th row As 15th row.
26th row P2, T3F, P3, C4FP, C4BP, P3, T3B, P2.
27th row As 13th row.
28th row P3, T3F, P4, C4F, P4, T3B, P3.
29th row As 11th row.
30th row P4, C4FP, P2, K4, P2, C4BP, P4.
31st row As 9th row.
32nd row P6, C4FP, C4F, C4BP, P6.
33rd row As 7th row.
34th row P8, C4FP, C4BP, P8.
35th and 36th rows As 1st and 2nd rows.
These 36 rows form the patt.

MATERIALS

11(12: 12) 50 g balls of Hayfield Pure Wool Classics DK in main colour, M.
1 ball in each of 2 contrast colours, A and B.
1 pair of 4 mm (No. 8/US 5) knitting needles.
1 cable needle.
3.75 mm (No. 9/US 4) crochet hook.
5 buttons.

MEASUREMENTS

To fit Bust	86 cm (91: 97)	34 ins (36: 38)
Actual measure-ment	107 cm (112: 117)	42 ins (44: 46)
Length to shoulder	50 cm (51: 52)	19¾ ins (20: 20½)
Sleeve seam	43 cm (44: 44)	17 ins (17¼: 17¼)

TENSION

22 sts and 28 rows to 10 cm (4 ins) over st st using 4 mm (No. 8/US 5) needles.

ABBREVIATIONS

C4B–sl next 2 sts to cn to back of work, K2, then K2 from cn; C4F–sl next 2 sts to cn to front of work, K2, then K2 from cn; C4BP–sl next 2 sts to cn to back of work, K2, then P2 from cn; C4FP–sl next 2 sts to cn to front of work, P2, then K2 from cn; T3B–sl next st to cn to back of work, K2, then P1 from cn; T3F–sl next 2 sts to cn to front of work, P1, then K2 from cn; T2R–K into front of 2nd st on left-hand needle, then K into front of first st allowing both sts to fall from needle; T2L–K into back of 2nd st on left-hand needle, then K into front of first st allowing both sts to fall from needle; dc–double crochet; ch–chain. Also see page 10.

BACK

With 4 mm (No. 8/US 5) needles and M, cast on 150(158: 166) sts.
Foundation row (WS) P to end.
1st row K1, [T2R, T2L] to last st, K1.
2nd row P to end.
3rd row K1, [T2L, T2R] to last st, K1.
4th row P to end.
These 4 rows form the rep of Honeycombe patt, work 12 more rows. **
Dec row Patt 13(13: 9), [K2 tog, T2L, K2 tog, patt 6] 10(11: 12) times, K2 tog, patt to end. 129(135: 141) sts.
* Cont in patt as folls:
1st row K 27(29: 31), [work 24 sts as 1st row of Panel A, K 27(29: 31)] twice.
2nd row P 27(29: 31), [work 24 sts as 2nd row of Panel A, P 27(29: 31)] twice. *
This sets position of patt. Keeping Panel sts correct throughout and rem sts in reverse st st, cont until the 36 rows are complete.
Dec row K 33(35: 33), [K2 tog] twice, P1, P2 tog, P1, [K2 tog] twice, K 39(41: 43), [K2 tog] twice, P1, P2 tog, P1, [K2 tog] twice, K to end. 119(125: 131) sts.
Beg with a P row, work 14 rows in reverse st st.
Inc row P 34(36: 38), m1, P1, m1, P2, m1, P1, m1, P1, m1, P 41(43: 45), m1, P1, m1, P1, m1, P2, m1, P1, m1, P to end. 129(135: 141) sts.
Rep from * to * once more.
This sets position of patt. Keeping Panel sts correct throughout and rem sts in reverse st st, cont until the 10th row of Panel A is complete.

Shape Armholes

Keeping patt correct, cast off 5(6: 7) sts at beg of next 2 rows, then dec one st at each end of next 9 rows. 101(105: 109) sts.
Cont without shaping until the 36 rows are complete.
Inc row K 10(2: 4), m1, [K 4(5: 5), m1] 20 times, K to end. 122(126: 130) sts.
Cont in Honeycombe patt as at beg

until work meas 49(50: 51) cm [19¼(19¾: 20) ins] from beg, ending with a WS row.

Shape Shoulders
Keeping patt correct cast off 13 sts at beg of next 4 rows, then 12(13: 14) sts at beg of foll 2 rows.
Cast off rem 46(48: 50) sts.

LEFT FRONT

With 4 mm (No. 8/US 5) needles and M, cast on 74(78: 82) sts and work as given for Back to **.
Dec row Patt 13(9: 9), [K2 tog, T2L, K2 tog, patt 6] 4(5: 5) times, K2 tog, patt to end. 65(67: 71) sts.
*** Cont in patt as folls:
1st row K 14(14: 16), work 24 sts as 1st row of Panel A, K to end.
2nd row P 27(29: 31), work 24 sts as 2nd row of Panel A, P to end. ***
This sets position of patt. Keeping Panel sts correct throughout and rem sts in reverse st st, cont until the 36 rows are complete.
Dec row K 20(20: 22), [K2 tog] twice, P1, P2 tog, P1, [K2 tog] twice, K to end. 60(62: 66) sts.
Beg with a P row, work 14 rows in reverse st st.
Inc row P 34(36: 38), m1, P1, m1, P2, m1, P1, m1, P1, m1, P to end. 65(67: 71) sts.
Rep from *** to *** once more.
This sets position of patt. Keeping Panel sts correct throughout and rem sts in reverse st st, cont until the 11th row of Panel A is complete.

Shape Armhole
Keeping patt correct, cast off 5(6: 7) sts at beg of next row, then dec one st at armhole edge on next 9 rows. 51(52: 55) sts.
Cont without shaping until the 36 rows are complete.
Inc row K 1(3: 3), m1, [K 8(5: 5), m1] 6(9: 10) times, K to end. 58(62: 66) sts.
Cont in Honeycombe patt as at beg of Back until work meas 43(44: 45) cm [17(17¼: 17¾) ins] from beg, ending with a RS row.

Shape Neck
Keeping patt correct, cast off 8(9: 10) sts at beg of next row, then 3 sts at beg of foll 2 alt rows.
Dec one st at neck edge on next 6(8: 10) rows. 38(39: 40) sts.
Cont without shaping until work meas same as Back to shoulders, ending with a WS row.

Shape Shoulder
Keeping patt correct, cast off 13 sts at beg of next and foll alt row.
Work 1 row straight, then cast off rem 12(13: 14) sts.

RIGHT FRONT

With 4 mm (No. 8/US 5) needles and M, cast on 74(78: 82) sts and work as given for Back to **.
Dec row Patt 13(9: 9), [K2 tog, T2L, K2 tog, patt 6] 4(5: 5) times, K2 tog, patt to end. 65(67: 71) sts.
**** Cont in patt as folls:
1st row K 27(29: 31), work 24 sts as 1st row of Panel A, K to end.
2nd row P 14(14: 16), work 24 sts as 2nd row of Panel A, P to end. ****
This sets position of patt. Keeping Panel sts correct throughout and rem sts in reverse st st, cont until the 36 rows are complete.
Dec row K 33(35: 37), [K2 tog] twice, P1, P2 tog, P1, [K2 tog] twice, K to end. 60(62: 66) sts.
Beg with a P row, work 14 rows in reverse st st.
Inc row P 21(21: 23), m1, P1, m1, P1, m1, P2, m1, P1, m1, P to end. 65(67: 71) sts.
Rep from **** to **** once more.
This sets position of patt. Keeping Panel sts correct throughout and rem sts in reverse st st, cont until the 10th row of Panel A is complete.

Shape Armhole
Keeping patt correct, cast off 5(6: 7) sts at beg of next row. Work 1 row straight.
Dec one st at armhole edge on next 9 rows. 51(52: 55) sts.
Cont to match Left Front, reversing all shaping.

SLEEVES

With 4 mm (No. 8/US 5) needles and M, cast on 82 sts and work as given for Back to **.
Dec row Patt 5, [K2 tog, patt 6, K2 tog, T2L] 6 times, patt 5. 70 sts.
Cont in patt as folls:
1st row K23, work 24 sts as 1st row of Panel A, K23.
2nd row P23, work 24 sts as 2nd row of Panel A, P23.

This sets position of patt. Keeping Panel sts correct throughout and rem sts in reverse st st, cont until the 36 rows are complete, *at the same time,* inc one st at each end of the 5th and every foll 6th row. 80 sts.
Dec row K34, [K2 tog] twice, P4, [K2 tog] twice, K34. 75 sts.
Cont in reverse st st still inc on every 6th row as set until there are 91(93: 95) sts.
Cont without shaping work until meas 42(43: 43) cm [16½(17: 17) ins] from beg, ending with a K row.

Shape Top
Cast off 5(6: 7) sts at beg of next 2 rows.
Dec one st at each end of next and every foll 4th row until 75(73: 71) sts rem, then every foll alt row until 49 sts rem. Work 1 row straight.
Cast off 2 sts at beg of next 12 rows.
Cast off rem 25 sts.

TO MAKE UP

Press work lightly on WS according to instructions on ball band, taking care not to flatten patt.
Using B and Bullion st, embroider 4 rose motifs (work 5 outer petals, twisting yarn 9 times round needle, then 2 centre petals, twisting yarn 5 times round needle) to each patt Panel A, working one at top and bottom of each "diamond" and one at each side.
Using B embroider 3 French Knots to small centre cable, inside small centre "diamond" of each patt Panel A.
Using A and Lazy Daisy st embroider leaves in groups of 3, one each side of small centre cable and 3 along each edge of large "diamond" of each patt Panel A, between rose motifs.
Using A and Lazy Daisy st embroider one larger leaf to each side of rose motifs placed at tip of large "diamond" furthest away from Honeycombe st.
Using A and Chain st embroider lines above or below each section of Honeycombe st on welt, cuffs and yoke.
With 3.75 mm (No. 9/US 4) crochet hook, M and RS facing, work 51dc along cast on edge of sleeve, turn.
Break off M and join in A.
2nd row Work 1dc into each dc to end, turn.
3rd row 1ch, miss first dc, 1 dc into each dc to end.

Break off A and join in B.

With RS facing, miss first dc, * [work 1 long dc, 2ch, 1 long dc] all into next st 3 rows below, miss 2dc; rep from * to end.

Fasten off.

Join shoulder seams. Join side seams. With 3.75 mm (No. 9/US 4) crochet hook, M and RS facing beg at left side seam, work 94(97: 100) dc along cast on edge of back and 48(51: 54) dc along cast on edge of right front, work 1 dc into corner and mark this st, work 73(75: 77) dc up right front edge and 1 dc into corner and mark this st, work 21(22: 23) dc up right front neck, 30(32: 34) dc across back neck and 21(22: 23) dc down left front neck, work 1 dc into corner and mark this st, work 73(75: 77) dc down left front edge and 1 dc into corner and mark this st, then work 48 (51: 54) dc along cast on edge of left front.

Break off M and join in A.

Work 2 rows in dc, working 3 dc into each marked st.

Break off A and join in B.

With RS facing, miss first dc, * [work 1 long dc, 2ch, 1 long dc] all into next st 3 rows below, miss 2 dc; rep from * to end.

Fasten off.

Join ends of edging.

Sew in sleeves, making a pleat at top each side of shoulder seam. Join sleeve seams.

Press seams lightly on WS.

With 3.75 mm (No. 9/US 4) crochet hook and A, make 5 buttonloops spaced evenly along front edge.

Sew on buttons.

TARTAN MOHAIR WRAP

MATERIALS

10 × 50 g balls of Hayfield Mohair Fancy in main colour, M.
4 × 50 g balls of Hayfield Mohair in each of 2 contrast colours, A and B.
3 balls in 3rd contrast colour, C.
$5\frac{1}{2}$ mm (No. 5/US 8) circular needle, 100 cm OR 42 ins long.

MEASUREMENTS

| Width | 114 cm | 45 ins |
| Length | 145 cm | 57 ins |

TENSION

19 sts and 22 rows to 10 cm (4 ins) over moss st using $5\frac{1}{2}$ mm (No. 5/US 8) needles.

ABBREVIATIONS

See page 10.

NOTE

When working patt from Chart read WS rows from right to left and RS rows from left to right. Use a separate length of yarn for each section and twist yarns tog where they join on every row to avoid a hole.

TO MAKE

With $5\frac{1}{2}$ mm (No. 5/US 8) circular needle and M, cast on 215 sts.
Work 9 rows in garter st.
Cont in patt as folls:
1st row (WS) K8M, [K1A, P1M] 6 times, [K1M, P1C] twice, K1M, * [P1B, K1M] 6 times, [P1M, K1C] twice, P1M, [K1A, P1M] 6 times, [K1M, P1C] twice, K1M; rep from * 4 times more, [P1B, K1M] 6 times, K8M.
2nd row K8M, [K1B, P1M] 6 times, * [K1C, P1M] twice, K1C, [P1A, K1M] 6 times, [P1C, K1M] twice, P1C, [K1B, P1M] 6 times; rep from * 4 times more, [K1C, P1M] twice, K1C, [P1A, K1M] 6 times, K8M.
This sets position of patt. Working throughout in moss st BUT keeping 8 sts at each end of every row in garter st in M, beg with row 3 cont in patt from Chart starting and ending rows as indicated until the 30 rows are complete.
Rep these 30 rows 9 times more.
Cont in M only:
Work 9 rows in garter st.
Cast off *loosely* knitwise.
Do not press.

KEY

☐ M
• A
⊚ B
⊠ C

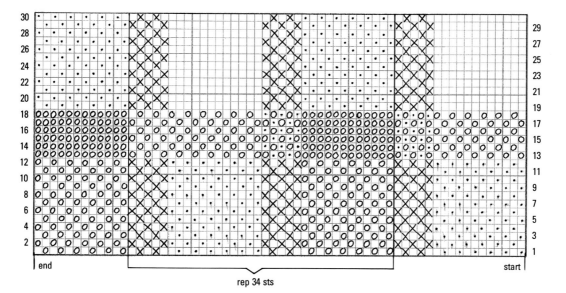

rep 34 sts

end · · · · · · · · · start

FISHERMAN'S ARAN SHIRT

MATERIALS

12(15: 25: 27: 29) 50 g balls of Hayfield Brig Aran Classics.
1 pair each of 3¾ mm (No. 9/US 4), 4 mm (No. 8/US 5) and 4½ mm (No. 7/US 6) knitting needles.
Set of four 4 mm (No. 8/US 5) double-pointed needles.
1 cable needle.

MEASUREMENTS

To fit Chest	66–71 cm	26–28 ins
	(76–81:	(30–32:
	86–91:	34–36:
	97–102:	38–40:
	107–112)	42–44)
Length to shoulder	44 cm	17¼ ins
	(56:	(22:
	66:	26:
	68:	26¾:
	70)	27½)
Sleeve seam	28 cm	11 ins
	(37:	(14½:
	46:	18:
	47:	18½:
	48)	19)

TENSION

19 sts and 25 rows to 10 cm (4 ins) over st st using 4½ mm (No. 7/US 6) needles.

ABBREVIATIONS

LT–K into back of 2nd st on left-hand needle, then K into back of first st allowing both sts to fall from needle; RT–K2 tog leaving sts on left-hand needle, then K into first st again allowing both sts to fall from needle; BC–sl next st to cn to back of work, K2, then P1 from cn; FC–sl next 2 sts to cn to front of work, P1, then K2 from cn; C3–sl next 2 sts to cn to front of work, K1, then K2 from cn; C4B–sl next 2 sts to cn to back of work, K2, then K2 from cn; C4F–sl next 2 sts to cn to front of work, K2, then K2 from cn; C6B–sl next 3 sts to cn to back of work, K3, then K3 from cn; C6F–sl next 3 sts to cn to front of work, K3, then K3 from cn; MB–pick up loop lying between sts and [K1, P1, K1] into it, turn, P3, turn, sl 1, K2 tog, psso. Also see page 10.

PANEL A

1st row K5, P2.
2nd row FC, P4.
3rd row K4, P2, K1.
4th row K1, FC, P3.
5th row K3, P2, K1, P1.
6th row P1, K1, FC, P2.
7th row K2, P2, K1, P1, K1.
8th row K1, P1, K1, FC, P1.
9th row K1, P2, [K1, P1] twice.
10th row [P1, K1] twice, FC.
11th row P1, [P1, K1] 3 times.
12th row [K1, P1] twice, BC.
13th row As 9th row.
14th row P1, K1, P1, BC, P1.
15th row As 7th row.
16th row K1, P1, BC, P2.
17th row As 5th row.
18th row P1, BC, P3.
19th row As 3rd row.
20th row BC, P4.
These 20 rows form the rep of patt.

PANEL B

1st row P2, K5.
2nd row P4, BC.
3rd row K1, P2, K4.
4th row P3, BC, K1.
5th row P1, K1, P2, K3.
6th row P2, BC, K1, P1.
7th row [K1, P1] twice, P1, K2.
8th row P1, BC, K1, P1, K1.
9th row [P1, K1] twice, P2, K1.
10th row BC, [K1, P1] twice.
11th row [K1, P1] 3 times, P1.
12th row FC, [P1, K1] twice.
13th row As 9th row.
14th row P1, FC, P1, K1, P1.
15th row As 7th row.
16th row P2, FC, P1, K1.
17th row As 5th row.
18th row P3, FC, P1.
19th row As 3rd row.
20th row P4, FC.
These 20 rows form the rep of patt.

PANEL C

1st and every foll alt row K1, P8, K1.
2nd row P1, C4B, C4F, P1.
4th row P1, K8, P1.
6th row P1, C4F, C4B, P1.
8th row As 4th row.
These 8 rows form the rep of patt.

PANEL D

1st row K1, P4, K1.
2nd row P1, K4, P1.
3rd row As 1st row.
4th row P1, C4F, P1.
These 4 rows form the rep of patt.

PANEL E

1st row K1, P4, K1.
2nd row P1, K4, P1.
3rd row As 1st row.
4th row P1, C4B, P1.
These 4 rows form the rep of patt.

PANEL F

1st row K3, P2, K3, P4, K3, P2, K3.
2nd row [P2, BC] twice, [FC, P2] twice.
3rd row [K2, P2, K3, P2] twice, K2.
4th row P1, [BC, P2] twice, FC, P2, FC, P1.
5th row K1, P2, K3, P2, K4, P2, K3, P2, K1.
6th row [BC, P2] twice, MB, P1, pass st from bobble over this st, P1, FC, P2, FC.
7th row P2, K3, P2, K6, P2, K3, P2.
8th row [FC, P2] twice, [P2, BC] twice.
9th row As 5th row.
10th row P1, [FC, P2] twice, BC, P2, BC, P1.
11th row As 3rd row.
12th row [P2, FC] twice, [BC, P2] twice.
These 12 rows form the rep of patt.

PANEL G

1st row K1, P6, K1.
2nd row P1, K6, P1.
3rd row As 1st row.
4th row P1, C6F, P1.
5th–8th rows Rep 1st and 2nd rows twice.
These 8 rows form the rep of patt.

PANEL H

1st row K1, P6, K1.
2nd row P1, K6, P1.
3rd row As 1st row.
4th row P1, C6B, P1.
5th–8th rows Rep 1st and 2nd rows twice.
These 8 rows form the rep of patt.

PANEL J

1st row P2, K6, P4, [K1, P1] 3 times, P4, K3.
2nd row P2, BC, FC, [K1, P1] twice, BC, C3, P4, BC.
3rd row K1, P2, K4, P3, K1, P2, [K1, P1] twice, [P2, K2] twice.
4th row P1, BC, P2, FC, K1, P1, BC, K1, P1, C3, P2, BC, P1.
5th row [K2, P2] twice, [P1, K1] twice, P2, K1, P3, K4, P2, K1.
6th row BC, P4, FC, BC, [K1, P1] twice, C3, BC, P2.
7th row K3, P5, [K1, P1] 3 times, P3, K6, P2.

8th row K2, P6, C4B, [K1, P1] 3 times, C4B, P3.
9th row K3, P4, [K1, P1] 3 times, P4, K6, P2.
10th row FC, P4, BC, C3, [K1, P1] twice, BC, FC, P2.
11th row [K2, P2] twice, [K1, P1] twice, P3, K1, P2, K4, P2, K1.
12th row P1, FC, P2, BC, K1, P1, C3, K1, P1, BC, P2, FC, P1.
13th row K1, P2, K4, P2, K1, P4, K1, P1, K1, [P2, K2] twice.
14th row P2, FC, BC, [K1, P1] twice, C3, BC, P4, FC.
15th row P2, K6, P5, [K1, P1] 3 times, P3, K3.
16th row P3, C4F, [K1, P1] 3 times, C4F, P6, K2.
These 16 rows form the rep of patt.

BACK AND FRONT (alike)

With 4 mm (No. 8/US 5) needles cast on 97(122: 137: 147: 152) sts.
1st row (RS) K2, [K1, P2, K2] to end.
2nd row P2, [K2, P3] to end.
3rd row K2, [LT, P1, K2] to end.
4th row P2, [K1, P1, K1, P2] to end.
5th row K2, [P1, LT, K2] to end.
6th row P2, [P1, K2, P2] to end.
7th row K2, [P1, RT, K2] to end.
8th row As 4th row.
9th row K2, [RT, P1, K2] to end.
10th row As 2nd row.
Rows 3–10 form the rep of patt. Cont until work meas 12(14: 16: 17: 18) cm [4¾(5½: 6¼: 6¾: 7) ins] from beg, ending with a RS row.
Work 4 rows in garter st, inc 4(3: 6: 8: 7) sts evenly across the last row. 101(125: 143: 155: 159) sts.
Change to 4½ mm (No. 7/US 6) needles and cont in patt as folls:
1st row K1, [P1, K1] 1(2: 3: 6: 7) times, work 0(0: 7: 7: 7) sts as 1st row of Panel A, work 0(10: 10: 10: 10) sts as 1st row of Panel C, work 6 sts as 1st row of Panel E, work 20 sts as 1st row of Panel F, work 8 sts as 1st row of Panel H, K1, work 25 sts as 1st row of Panel J, K1, work 8 sts as 1st row of Panel G, work 20 sts as 1st row of Panel F, work 6 sts as 1st row of Panel D, work 0 (10: 10: 10: 10) sts as 1st row of Panel C, work 0(0: 7: 7: 7) sts as 1st row of Panel B, K1, [P1, K1] to end.
2nd row P1, [K1, P1] 1(2: 3: 6: 7) times, work 0(0: 7: 7: 7) sts as 2nd row of Panel B, work 0(10: 10: 10: 10) sts as 2nd row of Panel C, work 6 sts as 2nd row of Panel D, work 20 sts as 2nd

row of Panel F, work 8 sts as 2nd row of Panel G, P1, work 25 sts as 2nd row of Panel J, P1, work 8 sts as 2nd row of Panel H, work 20 sts as 2nd row of Panel F, work 6 sts as 2nd row of Panel E, work 0 (10: 10: 10: 10) sts as 2nd row of Panel C, work 0(0: 7: 7: 7) sts as 2nd row of Panel A, P1, [K1, P1] to end.
Keeping Panel sts correct throughout and rem sts as set, cont as folls:
3rd row P1, [K1, P1] 1(2: 3: 6: 7) times, patt to last 3(5: 7: 13: 15) sts, P1, [K1, P1] to end.
4th row K1, [P1, K1] 1(2: 3: 6: 7) times, patt to last 3(5: 7: 13: 15) sts, K1, [P1, K1] to end.
These 4 rows form the rep of Irish Moss st at each end. Keeping Panel sts correct and rem sts as set, cont until work meas 39(51: 61: 63: 65) cm [15¼(20: 24: 24¾: 25½) ins] from beg, ending with a WS row.

Shape Top
Cast off 33(44: 52: 57: 58) sts at beg of next 2 rows.
Leave rem 35(37: 39: 41: 43) sts on a holder for collar.

SLEEVES

With 3¾ mm (No. 9/US 4) needles cast on 42(47: 47: 52: 52) sts and work 5(6: 8: 8: 8) cm [2(2¼: 3¼: 3¼: 3¼) ins] in patt as for Body welt, ending with a RS row. Work 3 rows in garter st.
Inc row K 1(4: 11: 2: 12), m1, [K 4(3: 1: 2: 1), m1] 10(13: 25: 24: 28) times, K to end. 53(61: 73: 77: 81) sts.
Change to 4½ mm (No. 7/US 6) needles and cont in patt as folls:
1st row K1, [P1, K1] 2(4: 2: 3: 4) times, work 0(0: 10: 10: 10) sts as 1st row of Panel C, work 8 sts as 1st row of Panel H, K1, work 25 sts as 1st row of Panel J, K1, work 8 sts as 1st row of Panel G, work 0(0: 10: 10: 10) sts as 1st row of Panel C, K1, [P1, K1] to end.
2nd row P1, [K1, P1] 2(4: 2: 3: 4) times, work 0(0: 10: 10: 10) sts as 2nd row of Panel C, work 8 sts as 2nd row of Panel G, P1, work 25 sts as 2nd row of Panel J, P1, work 8 sts as 2nd row of Panel H, work 0(0: 10: 10: 10) sts as 2nd row of Panel C, P1, [K1, P1] to end.
This sets position of patt. Keeping Panel sts correct throughout and rem sts as set, *at the same time*, inc one st at each end of next and every foll 3rd row working inc sts into Irish Moss st,

until there are 83(95: 107: 119: 131) sts.
Cont without shaping until work meas
28(37: 46: 47: 48) cm [11(14½: 18: 18½:
19) ins] from beg, ending with a WS
row.

Shape Top

Keeping patt correct, cast off 27(33:
39: 45: 51) sts at beg of next 2 rows.
29 sts.
Place a marker at each end of last row.
Cont in patt as set until work meas
12(16: 19: 20: 21) cm [4¾(6¼: 7½: 7¾:
8¼) ins] from markers, ending with a
WS row and dec 4 sts evenly across last
row.
Leave rem 25 sts on a holder.

COLLAR

Sew sleeve tops above markers to cast
off sts of back and front.
With set of four 4 mm (No. 8/US 5)
needles and RS facing, K 34(36: 38: 40:
42) sts of back from holder, K next st
tog with first st of left sleeve, K 23 sts
from holder, K next st tog with first st
of front, K 33(35: 37: 39: 41) sts from
holder, K next st tog with first st of
right sleeve, K 23 sts from holder, K
next st tog with first st of back.
116(120: 124: 128: 132) sts.
Work 8(8: 10: 10: 10) cm [3¼(3¼: 4: 4:
4) ins] in rounds of K2, P2 rib.
Cast off *loosely* in rib.

TO MAKE UP

Do not press.
Sew in sleeves. Join side and sleeve
seams.
Press seams lightly on WS according
to instructions on ball band.

GUERNSEY SWEATER

MATERIALS

5(8: 13: 15) 50 g balls of Hayfield
Raw Cotton Classics DK.
1 pair each of 3¼ mm (No. 10/US 3)
and 4 mm (No. 8/US 5) knitting
needles.
1 cable needle.

MEASUREMENTS

To fit Chest/ Bust	46–56 cm (66–76: 86–97: 107–112)	18–22 ins (26–30: 34–38: 42–44)
All round approx.	63 cm (86: 112: 134)	25 ins (34: 44: 53)
Length to shoulder	35 cm (57: 66: 72)	13¾ ins (22½: 26: 28¼)
Sleeve seam	24 cm (36: 45: 47)	9½ ins (14¼: 17¾: 18½)

TENSION

22 sts and 28 rows to 10 cm (4 ins)
over st st using 4 mm (No. 8/US 5)
needles.

ABBREVIATIONS

C4–sl next 2 sts to cn to front of
work, K2, then K2 from cn. Also
see page 10.

PANEL A

1st row K1, P2, K9.
2nd row P8, K2, P2.
3rd row K3, P2, K7.
4th row P6, K2, P4.
5th row K5, P2, K5.
6th row P4, K2, P6.
7th row K7, P2, K3.
8th row P2, K2, P8.
9th row K9, P2, K1.
10th row As 8th row.
11th row As 7th row.
12th row As 6th row.
13th row As 5th row.
14th row As 4th row.
15th row As 3rd row.
16th row As 2nd row.
These 16 rows form the rep of patt.

PANEL B

1st row P11.
2nd row P11.
3rd and 4th rows As 1st and 2nd
rows.
5th row K5, P1, K5.
6th row P4, K1, P1, K1, P4.
7th row K3, [P1, K1] twice, P1, K3.
8th row P2, [K1, P1] 3 times, K1, P2.
9th row K1, [P1, K1] to end.
10th row As 8th row.
11th row As 7th row.
12th row As 6th row.
13th row As 5th row.
14th row P11.
These 14 rows form the rep of patt.

PANEL C

1st row P2, K4, P2.
2nd row K2, P4, K2.
3rd row P2, C4, P2.
4th row As 2nd row.
5th and 6th rows As 1st and 2nd
rows.
These 6 rows form the rep of patt.

PANEL D

1st row K17.
2nd row P17.
3rd row K17.
4th row P8, K1, P8.
5th row K7, P1, K1, P1, K7.
6th row P6, [K1, P1] 3 times, P5.
7th row K5, [P1, K1] 4 times, K4.
8th row P4, [K1, P1] 5 times, P3.
9th row K3, [P1, K1] 6 times, K2.
10th row P2, [K1, P1] 7 times, P1.
11th row K1, [P1, K1] 8 times
12th row As 10th row.
13th row As 9th row.
14th row As 8th row.
15th row As 7th row.
16th row As 6th row.
17th row As 5th row.
18th row As 4th row.
19th row As 1st row.
20th row As 2nd row.
21st row P17.
22nd row As 2nd row.
23rd row As 21st row.
24th row As 2nd row.
These 24 rows form the rep of patt.

PANEL E

1st row K 12(12: 14: 14).
2nd row P 12(12: 14: 14).
3rd row K 9(9: 10: 10), P2, K 1(1: 2: 2).
4th row P 2(2: 3: 3), K2, P 8(8: 9: 9).
5th row K 7(7: 8: 8), P2, K 3 (3: 4: 4).
6th row P 4(4: 5: 5), K2, P 6(6: 7: 7).
7th row K 5(5: 6: 6), P2, K 5(5: 6: 6).
8th row P 6(6: 7: 7), K2, P 4(4: 5: 5).
9th row K 3(3: 4: 4), P2, K 7(7: 8: 8).
10th row P 8(8: 9: 9), K2, P 2(2: 3: 3).
11th row K 1(1: 2: 2), P2, K 9(9: 10: 10).
12th row As 2nd row.
Rows 3–12 form the rep of patt.

PANEL F

1st row K 12(12: 14: 14).
2nd row P 12(12: 14: 14).
3rd row K 1(1: 2: 2), P2, K 9(9: 10: 10).
4th row P 8(8: 9: 9), K2, P 2(2: 3: 3).
5th row K 3(3: 4: 4), P2, K 7(7: 8: 8).
6th row P 6(6: 7: 7), K2, P 4(4: 5: 5).
7th row K 5(5: 6: 6), P2, K 5(5: 6: 6).
8th row P 4(4: 5: 5), K2, P 6(6: 7: 7).
9th row K 7(7: 8: 8), P2, K 3(3: 4: 4).
10th row P 2(2: 3: 3), K2, P 8(8: 9: 9).
11th row K 9(9: 10: 10), P2, K 1(1: 2: 2).
12th row As 2nd row.
Rows 3–12 form the rep of patt.

PANEL G

1st row K 17(19).
2nd row P 17(19).
3rd row K 1(2), [P1, K1] 8 times, K 0(1).
4th row P 2(3), [K1, P1] 7 times, P 1(2).
5th row K 3(4), [P1, K1] 6 times, K 2(3).
6th row P 4(5), [K1, P1] 5 times, P 3(4).
7th row K 5(6), [P1, K1] 4 times, K 4(5).
8th row P 6(7), [K1, P1] 3 times, P 5(6).
9th row K 7(8), [P1, K1] twice, K 6(7).
10th row P 8(9), K1, P 8(9).
11th row As 1st row.
12th row As 2nd row.
13th row P 17(19).
14th row As 2nd row.
15th row As 13th row.
16th row As 2nd row.
These 16 rows form the rep of patt.

BACK

With 3¼ mm (No. 10/US 3) needles cast on 62(86: 110: 134) sts.
1st row (RS) P2, K1, * work 8 sts as 1st row of Panel C, [K1, P2] 5 times, K1; rep from * to last 11 sts, work 8 sts as 1st row of Panel C, K1, P2.
2nd row K2, P1, * work 8 sts as 2nd row of Panel C, [P1, K2] 5 times, P1; rep from * to last 11 sts, work 8 sts as 2nd row of Panel C, P1, K2.
This sets position of patt. Keeping Panel sts correct throughout and rem sts in rib, cont until 11(17: 23: 29) rows in all have been worked.
Inc row [Patt 7, m1, patt 9, m1, patt 6, m1, patt 2] 2(3: 4: 5) times, patt 7, m1, patt 7. 69(96: 123: 150) sts.
Change to 4 mm (No. 8/US 5) needles and cont in patt as folls:
1st row [P2, work 11 sts as 1st row of Panel B, P2, work 12 sts as 1st row of Panel A] 2(3: 4: 5) times P2, work 11 sts as 1st row of Panel B, P2.
2nd row [K2, work 11 sts as 2nd row of Panel B, K2, work 12 sts as 2nd row of Panel A] 2(3: 4: 5) times, K2, work 11 sts as 2nd row of Panel B, K2.
This sets position of patt. Keeping Panel sts correct throughout and rem sts as set, cont until 39(59: 79: 99) rows in all have been worked from beg, thus ending with a 13th patt row of Panel B.
Next row [K2, P11, K2, P12] 2(3: 4: 5) times, K2, P11, K2.
P 3 rows.
Next row P to end dec 0(3: 0: 3) sts evenly across the row. 69(93: 123: 147) sts.
Cont in Diamond patt as folls:
1st row K3, [K1, P1, K4] to end.
2nd row P3, [K1, P1, K1, P3] to end.
3rd row P1, K1, P1, [K3, P1, K1, P1] to end.
4th row P1, K1, P1, [P4, K1, P1] to end.
5th row As 3rd row.
6th row As 2nd row.
7th row As 1st row.
8th row P to end.
P 3 rows.
Next row P to end inc 4 sts evenly across the row. 73(97: 127: 151) sts.
Cont in Yoke patt as folls:
1st row On 2nd, 3rd and 4th sizes only; [K 0(0: 1), work 8 sts as 1st row of Panel C] 0 (1: 2) times, work 12(17: 19) sts as 1st row of Panel F(G: G): On all sizes; work 8 sts as 1st row of Panel C, work 12(12: 14: 14) sts as 1st row of Panel E, work 8 sts as 1st row of Panel

C, work 17 sts as 1st row of Panel D, work 8 sts as 1st row of Panel C, work 12(12: 14: 14) sts as 1st row of Panel F, work 8 sts as 1st row of Panel C: On 2nd, 3rd and 4th sizes only; work 12(17: 19) sts as 1st row of Panel E(G: G), [work 8 sts as 1st row of Panel C, K 0(0: 1)] 0(1: 2) times.

This sets position of patt. Keeping Panel sts correct throughout and rem sts as set, cont until work meas 35(57: 66: 72) cm [13¾(22½: 26: 28¼) ins] from beg, ending with a WS row.

Shape Shoulders
Cast off 20(31: 44: 54) sts at beg of next 2 rows.
Leave rem 33(35: 39: 43) sts on a holder for neckband.

FRONT

Work as given for Back until front meas 29(50: 58: 64) cm [11½(19¾: 22¾: 25¼) ins] from beg, ending with a WS row.

Shape Neck
Next row Patt 31(42: 56: 66), turn and leave rem sts on a spare needle.
Keeping patt correct, dec one st at neck edge on next 9 rows, then every foll alt row until 20(31: 44: 54) sts rem.
Cont without shaping until work meas same as Back to shoulders, ending with a WS row.
Cast off.
Return to sts on spare needle; with RS facing sl first 11(13: 15: 19) sts on to a holder for neckband rejoin yarn to neck edge and patt to end.
Cont to match first side, reversing shaping.

SLEEVES

With 3¼ mm (No. 10/US 3) needles cast on 35(41: 47: 53) sts.
1st row (RS) [P2, K1] 1(2: 3: 4) times, work 8 sts as 1st row of Panel C, [K1, P2] 4 times, K1, work 8 sts as 1st row of Panel C, [K1, P2] 1(2: 3: 4) times.
This sets position of patt. Keeping Panel sts correct throughout and rem sts in rib, cont until 11(23: 23: 29) rows in all have been worked.
Inc row Rib 0(0: 0: 3), [m1, rib 1] 0(0: 2: 2) times, [inc in next st] 0(0: 1: 1) time, [rib 1, m1] 0(2: 2: 2) times, patt 7(8: 8: 8), m1, patt 8, [m1, rib 1] twice, inc in next st, [rib 1, m1] twice, patt 8,

m1, patt 7(8: 8: 8), [m1, rib 1] 0(2: 2: 2) times, [inc in next st] 0(0: 1: 1) time, [rib 1, m1] 0(0: 2: 2) times, rib 0(0: 0: 3). 42(52: 64: 70) sts.

Change to 4 mm (No. 8/US 5) needles and cont in patt as folls:

1st row P 0(0: 0: 2), K 0(0: 0: 1), P 0(0: 2: 2), K 0(5: 9: 9), P2, work 11 sts as 1st row of Panel B, P2, work 12 sts as 1st row of Panel A, P2, work 11 sts as 1st row of Panel B, P2, K 0(1: 1: 1), P 0(2: 2: 2), K 0(2: 8: 9), P 0(0: 0: 2).

This sets position of patt. Keeping Panel sts correct throughout and rem sts as set, *at the same time*, inc one st at each end of the 6th and every foll 3rd (4th: 5th: 4th) row, working inc sts into panels to match lower half of Back until there are 64(70: 88: 100) sts. Work 5(3: 8: 7) rows straight, thus ending with a 14th patt row of Panel B.

Next row P to end dec one st in centre. 63(69: 87: 99) sts. P3 rows. Work 8 rows in Diamond patt as on Back, *at the same time*, inc one st at each end of the 3rd and 6th rows. 67(73: 91: 103) sts.

Next row P to end inc 4 sts evenly across the row. 71(77: 95: 107) sts. P3 rows.

On 2nd, 3rd and 4th sizes only

1st row K 2(9: 15) sts to position 1st row of Panel F(G: G), work 8 sts as 1st row of Panel C, work 12(14: 14) sts as 1st row of Panel E, work 8 sts as 1st row of Panel C, work 17 sts as 1st row of Panel D, work 8 sts as 1st row of Panel C, work 12(14: 14) sts as 1st row of Panel F, work 8 sts as 1st row of Panel C, K 2(9: 15) sts to position 1st row of Panel E(G: G).

This sets position of patt. Keeping Panel sts correct throughout, *at the same time*, inc one st at each end of the 2nd and every foll 4th (6th: 5th) row, working inc sts into panels as set. Cont without shaping until the 24th patt row of panel D is complete. On all sizes cast off *loosely*.

NECKBAND

Join right shoulder seam.

With 3¼ mm (No. 10/US 3) needles and RS facing, pick up and K 24(25: 28: 27) sts evenly down left front neck, K front neck sts from holder dec one st in centre, pick up and K 24(25: 28: 27) sts evenly up right front neck, then K back neck sts from holder dec one st in centre. 90(96: 108: 114) sts.

Next row K 0(0: 0: 1), P 0(1: 0: 1), [K2, P1] 0(0: 1: 1) time, work 8 sts as 2nd row of Panel C, [P1, K2] 5 times, P1, work 8 sts as 2nd row of Panel C, [P1, K2] 4(5: 7: 8) times, P1, work 8 sts as 2nd row of Panel C, [P1, K2] 5 times, P1, work 8 sts as 2nd row of Panel C, [P1, K2] 4(5: 6: 6) times, P 1(0: 1: 1), K 0 (0: 0: 1).

This sets position of patt. Keeping Panel sts correct throughout and rem sts in rib, cont until 12(14: 16: 18) rows in all have been worked.

Cast off *loosely* in patt.

TO MAKE UP

Do not press.

Join left shoulder and neckband seam. Sew in sleeves, with centre of sleeve to shoulder seam. Join side and sleeve seams. Fold neckband in half to inside and sl st.

CRICKET-STYLE SWEATER

PANEL A

1st row K 5(6: 7).
2nd row P 5(6: 7).
3rd row As 1st row.
4th row K 5(6: 7).
5th–8th rows Rep 1st and 2nd rows twice.
These 8 rows form the rep of patt.

PANEL B

1st row K9.
2nd row P4, K1, P4.
3rd row K3, P1, K1, P1, K3.
4th row P2, [K1, P1] 3 times, P1.
5th row K1, [P1, K1] 4 times.
6th row As 4th row.
7th row As 3rd row.
8th row As 2nd row.
These 8 rows form the rep of patt.

PANEL C

1st row P2, K8, P2.
2nd row K2, P8, K2.
3rd and 4th rows As 1st and 2nd rows.
5th row P2, C4F, C4B, P2.
6th row As 2nd row.
These 6 rows form the rep of patt.

BACK

With 3¼ mm (No. 10/US 5) needles cast on 115(119: 123) sts.
1st row (RS) K1, [P1, K1] to end.
2nd row P1, [K1, P1] to end.
Rep these 2 rows until work meas 8 cm (3¼ ins) from beg, ending with a RS row.
Inc row Rib 16(17: 18), m1, [rib 2, m1] 41(42: 43) times, rib to end. 157(162: 167) sts.
Change to 4 mm (No. 8/US 5) needles and cont in patt as folls:
1st row [Work 5(6: 7) sts as 1st row of Panel A, work 12 sts as 1st row of Panel C, work 9 sts as 1st row of Panel B, work 12 sts as 1st row of Panel C] 4 times, work 5(6: 7) sts as 1st row of Panel A.

2nd row [Work 5(6: 7) sts as 2nd row of Panel A, work 12 sts as 2nd row of Panel C, work 9 sts as 2nd row of Panel B, work 12 sts as 2nd row of Panel C] 4 times, work 5(6: 7) sts as 2nd row of Panel A.
This sets position of patt. Keeping Panel sts correct throughout cont until work meas 48(49: 50) cm [19(19¼: 19¾) ins] from beg, ending with a WS row.

Shape Armholes
Keeping patt correct cast off 5(6: 7) sts at beg of next 2 rows. 147(150: 153) sts.

MATERIALS

16(17: 17) 50 g balls of Hayfield Raw Cotton Classics DK.
1 pair each of 3¼ mm (No. 10/US 3) and 4 mm (No. 8/US 5) knitting needles.
1 cable needle.

MEASUREMENTS

To fit Bust/ Chest	86 cm (91: 97)	34 ins (36: 38)
All round approx.	114 cm (119: 124)	45 ins (47: 49)
Length to shoulder	72 cm (74: 76)	28¼ ins (29¼: 30)
Sleeve length	50 cm (52: 54)	19¾ ins (20½: 21¼)

TENSION

22 sts and 28 rows to 10 cm (4 ins) over st st using 4 mm (No. 8/US 5) needles.

ABBREVIATIONS

C4F–sl next 2 sts to cn to front of work, K2, then K2 from cn; C4B–sl next 2 sts to cn to back of work, K2, then K2 from cn. Also see page 10.

Cont without shaping until work meas 72(74: 76) cm [28¼(29¼: 30) ins] from beg, ending with a WS row.

Shape Shoulders
Keeping patt correct, cast off 25(25: 26) sts at beg of next 2 rows, then 25(26: 26) sts at beg of foll 2 rows.
Leave rem 47(48: 49) sts on a holder for neckband.

POCKET LININGS (make 2)

With 4 mm (No. 8/US 5) needles cast on 23 sts.
Beg with a K row, cont in st st until work meas 9 cm (3½ ins) from beg, ending with a P row and inc 5 sts evenly across the last row. 28 sts.
Leave sts on a holder.

FRONT

Work as given for Back until front meas 17 cm (6¾ ins) from beg, ending with a WS row.

Place Pockets
Next row Patt 25(27: 29), sl next 28 sts on to a holder, with RS facing patt across sts of first pocket lining, patt 51(52: 53), sl next 28 sts onto a holder, with RS facing patt across sts of 2nd pocket lining, patt to end.
Cont until work meas same as Back to armholes, ending with a WS row.

Shape Armholes
Keeping patt correct cast off 5(6: 7) sts at beg of next 2 rows. 147(150: 153) sts.

Divide for Neck
Next row Patt 73(75: 76), turn and leave rem sts on a spare needle.
Keeping patt correct, dec one st at neck edge on next and every foll alt row until 57(58: 62) sts rem, then every foll 3rd row until 50(51: 52) sts rem.
Cont without shaping until work meas same as Back to shoulders, ending with a WS row.

Shape Shoulder

Keeping patt correct cast off 25(25:
26) sts at beg of next row. Work 1 row
straight, then cast off rem 25(26:
26) sts.
Return to sts on spare needle; with RS
facing sl first 1(0: 1) st on to a safety
pin for neckband, rejoin yarn to neck
edge and patt to end.
Cont to match first side, reversing all
shaping.

SLEEVES

With 3¼ mm (No. 10/US 3) needles cast
on 51(53: 55) sts and work 8 cm (3¼ ins)
in rib as for Back welt, ending with a
RS row.
Inc row Rib 6(7: 8), m1, [rib 2, m1] 19
times, rib to end. 71(73: 75) sts.
Change to 4 mm (No. 8/US 5) needles
and cont in patt as folls:
1st row K 2(3: 4), * work 12 sts as 1st
row of Panel C, work 5(6: 7) sts as 1st
row of Panel A, work 12 sts as 1st row
of Panel C *, work 9 sts as 1st row of
Panel B; rep from * to * once more, K
to end.
2nd row P 2(3: 4), * work 12 sts as 2nd
row of Panel C, work 5(6: 7) sts as 2nd
row of Panel A, work 12 sts as 2nd
row of Panel C *, work 9 sts as 2nd
row of Panel B; rep from * to * once
more, P to end.
This sets position of patt. Keeping
Panel sts correct throughout, *at the
same time*, inc one st at each end of next
and every foll 3rd row, working inc sts
into panels to match Back until there
are 129(135: 139) sts.
Cont without shaping until work meas
50(52: 54) cm [19¾(20½: 21¼) ins] from
beg, ending with a WS row.
Cast off *loosely*.

NECKBAND

Join right shoulder seam.
With 3¼ mm (No. 10/US 3) needles and
RS facing, pick up and K 57(59: 61) sts
evenly down left front neck, one st
from centre front, pick up and K
57(59: 61) sts evenly up right front
neck, then K back neck sts from
holder dec 1(0: 1) st in centre. 161(167:
171) sts.
Next row [K1, P1] 50(52: 53) times,
K1, P2 tog, P1, P2 tog tbl, K1, [P1,
K1] to end.
Next row Work in rib as set to 2 sts
before centre front st, K2 tog tbl, K1,
K2 tog, rib to end.
Work 6 more rows as set, dec one st at
either side of centre front st on every
row.
Cast off in rib, still dec at centre front.

POCKET TOPS

With 3¼ mm (No. 10/US 3) needles and
RS facing, K to end across sts on
holder inc one st in centre. 29 sts.
Work 6 rows in rib as for Back welt.
Cast off in rib.

TO MAKE UP

Do not press.
Join left shoulder and neckband seam.
Sew in sleeves. Join side and sleeve
seams. Sew down pocket tops and
pocket linings.
Press seams lightly on WS according
to instructions on ball band, omitting
ribbing.

CHUNKY FAIR ISLE SWEATER

MATERIALS

5(8: 13: 15) 50 g balls of Hayfield
Grampian Chunky in main colour,
M.
2(3: 4: 4) balls in first contrast
colour, A.
2(2: 3: 4) balls in second contrast
colour, B.
2(2: 3: 3) balls in third contrast
colour, C.
1 ball in fourth contrast colour, D.
1 pair each of 5 mm (No. 6/US 7)
and 6 mm (No. 4/US 9) knitting
needles.
Set of four 5 mm (No. 6/US 7)
double-pointed needles.

MEASUREMENTS

To fit Chest/ Bust	66–71 cm	26–28 ins
	(76–81:	(30–32:
	86–97:	34–38:
	102–112)	40–44)
All round approx.	81 cm	32 ins
	(99:	(39:
	119:	47:
	140)	55)
Length to shoulder	48 cm	19 ins
	(56:	(22:
	64:	25¼:
	72)	28¼)
Sleeve with cuff back	24 cm	9½ ins
	(31:	(12¼:
	39:	15¼:
	41)	16¼)

TENSION

18 sts and 18 rows to 10 cm (4 ins)
over patt using 6 mm (No. 4/US 9)
needles.

ABBREVIATIONS

See page 10.

NOTE

When working patt from Chart
read odd rows (K) from right to left
and even rows (P) from left to
right. Strand yarn not in use *loosely*
across WS of work to keep fabric
elastic.

BACK

With 5 mm (No. 6/US 7) needles and
B, cast on 62(78: 90: 106) sts.
1st row (RS) K2, [P2, K2] to end.
Break off B and join in M.
2nd row P2, [K2, P2] to end.
Cont in rib as set until work meas 5 cm
(2 ins) from beg, ending with a RS
row.
Inc row Rib 1(3: 9: 3), m1, [rib 6(6: 4:
5), m1] 10(12: 18: 20) times, rib to end.
73(91: 109: 127) sts.
Change to 6 mm (No. 4/US 9) needles.
Beg with a K row and working in st st
throughout, cont in patt from Chart
starting and ending rows as indicated
until the 36 rows are complete.
Rep rows 9–36 until 77(93: 105: 121)
rows in all have been worked in st st.

Shape Shoulders

Cast off 25(32: 39: 46) sts at beg of next
2 rows.
Leave rem 23(27: 31: 35) sts on a
holder for collar.

FRONT

Work as given for Back until 64(78:
90: 106) rows in all have been worked
in st st.

Shape Neck

Next row Patt 30(38: 46: 54), turn and
leave rem sts on a spare needle.
Keeping patt correct, dec one st at
neck edge on next 5(6: 7: 8) rows.
25(32: 39: 46) sts.
Cont without shaping until 77(93: 105:
121) rows in all have been worked in st
st.
Cast off.
Return to sts on spare needle; with RS
facing sl first 13(15: 17: 19) sts on to a
holder for collar, rejoin yarns to neck
edge and patt to end.
Cont to match first side, reversing
shaping.

SLEEVES

With 5 mm (No. 6/US 7) needles and B, cast on 30(34: 34: 38) sts and work 10 cm (4 ins) in 2 colour rib as for Back welt, ending with a RS row.
Inc row Rib 3(2: 5: 4), m1, [rib 2(3: 2: 3), m1] 12(10: 12: 10) times, rib to end. 43(45: 47: 49) sts.
Change to 6 mm (No. 4/US 9) needles. Beg with a K row and working in st st throughout, cont in patt from Chart to match Back starting and ending rows as indicated, *at the same time*, inc one st at each end of the 3rd and every foll alt row, working inc sts into patt until there are 47(49: 53: 71) sts, then every foll 3rd row until there are 63(73: 87: 97) sts.
Cont without shaping until work meas 29(36: 44: 46) cm [11½(14¼: 17¼: 18) ins] from beg, ending with a P row.
Cast off *loosely*.

COLLAR

Join shoulder seams.
With set of four 5 mm (No. 6/US 7) needles, M and RS facing, K back neck sts from holder, pick up and K 14(15: 16: 17) sts evenly down left front neck, K front neck sts from holder, then pick up and K 14(15: 16: 17) sts evenly up right front neck. 64(72: 80: 88) sts.
Work 10 cm (4 ins) in rounds of K2, P2 rib.
Break off M and join in B.
Work 1 more round, then cast off *loosely* in rib.

TO MAKE UP

Press work lightly on WS according to instructions on ball band, omitting ribbing.
Sew in sleeves, with centre of sleeve to shoulder seam. Join side and sleeve seams.
Press seams.

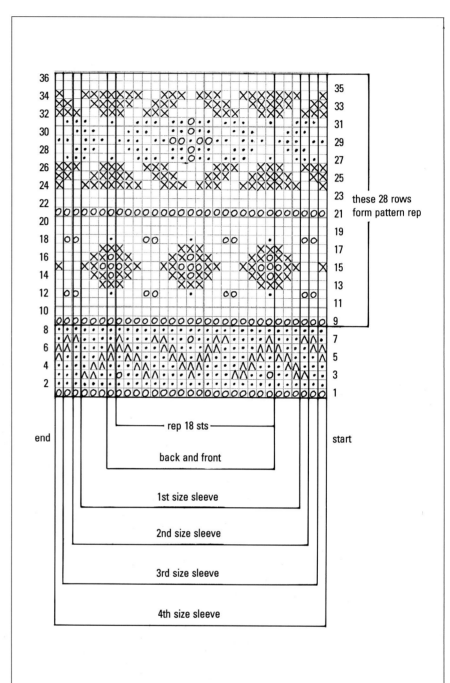

KEY

□ M
⊠ A
⊡ B
· C
△ D

SPORTY HIS AND HERS SWEATER

MATERIALS

17(19: 22) 50 g balls of Hayfield
Hedgerow Chunky Tweed.
1 pair each of 5½ mm (No. 5/US 8)
and 6½ mm (No. 3/US 10) knitting
needles.
1 cable needle.

MEASUREMENTS

To fit Bust/ Chest	86–91 cm (97–102: 107–112)	34–36 ins (38–40: 42–44)
All round approx.	117 cm (132: 148)	46 ins (52: 58)
Length to shoulder	66 cm (70: 74)	26 ins (27½: 29¼)
Sleeve seam	43 cm (46: 48)	17 ins (18: 19)

TENSION

14 sts and 19 rows to 10 cm (4 ins)
over st st using 6½ mm (No. 3/
US 10) needles.

ABBREVIATIONS

BC–sl next 2 sts to cn to back of
work, K2, then P2 from cn; FC–sl
next 2 sts to cn to front of work, P2,
then K2 from cn; T4B–sl next 3 sts
to cn to back of work, K1, then P1,
K1, P1 from cn; T4F–sl next st to
cn to front of work, K1, P1, K1,
then K1 from cn; C4B–sl next 2 sts
to cn to back of work, K2, then K2
from cn; C4F–sl next 2 sts to cn to
front of work, K2, then K2 from
cn; C8B–sl next 4 sts to cn to back
of work, K4, then K4 from cn;
C8F–sl next 4 sts to cn to front of
work, K4, then K4 from cn;
T3B–sl next st to cn to back of
work, K2, then P1 from cn; T3F–sl
next 2 sts to cn to front of work, P1,
then K2 from cn. Also see page 10.

PANEL A

1st row K9, P10, K9.
2nd row P9, C4B, K2, C4F, P9.
3rd row As 1st row.
4th row P7, BC, K2, C4B, FC, P7.
5th row K7, P2, K2, P6, K2, P2, K7.
6th row P5, BC, P1, T3B, K2, T3F,
P1, FC, P5.
7th row K5, P2, K3, [P2, K1] twice,
P2, K3, P2, K5.
8th row P3, BC, P2, T3B, P1, K2, P1,
T3F, P2, FC, P3.
9th row K3, P2, K4, [P2, K2] 3 times,
K2, P2, K3.
10th row P3, K2, P3, T3B, P2, K2, P2,
T3F, P3, K2, P3.
11th row K3, [P2, K3] 5 times.
12th row P3, FC, T3B, P3, K2, P3,
T3F, BC, P3.
13th row K5, P4, K4, P2, K4, P4, K5.
14th row P5, C4B, P4, K2, P4, C4F,
P5.
15th row As 13th row.
16th row P3, BC, FC, P2, K2, P2, BC,
FC, P3.
17th row As 9th row.
18th row P3, K2, P4, FC, K2, BC, P4,
K2, P3.
19th row K3, P2, K6, P6, K6, P2, K3.
20th row P3, FC, P4, C4F, K2, P4,
BC, P3.
21st row K5, P2, K4, P6, K4, P2, K5.
22nd row P5, FC, P2, K2, C4B, P2,
BC, P5.
23rd row As 5th row.
24th row P7, FC, C4F, K2, BC, P7.
These 24 rows form the rep of patt.

PANEL B

1st row P1, K1, P3, K1, P2.
2nd row T4B, T4F.
3rd row [P1, K1] 3 times, P2.
4th row [K1, P1] 3 times, K2.
5th row As 3rd row.
6th row As 4th row.
7th row As 3rd row.
8th row K1, P1, K3, P1, K2.
These 8 rows form the rep of patt.

PANEL C

1st row K2, P8, K2.
2nd row P2, C8B, P2.
3rd row As 1st row.
4th row P2, K8, P2.
5th row As 1st row.
6th row As 4th row.
7th row As 1st row.
8th row As 4th row.
These 8 rows form the rep of patt.

PANEL D

1st row K2, P8, K2.
2nd row P2, C8F, P2.
3rd row As 1st row.
4th row P2, K8, P2.
5th row As 1st row.
6th row As 4th row.
7th row As 1st row.
8th row As 4th row.
These 8 rows form the rep of patt.

PANEL E

1st row [K2, P4] twice.
2nd row C4F, P2, K4, P2.
3rd row As 1st row.
4th row [K4, P2] twice.
5th row As 1st row.
6th row K4, P2, C4F, P2.
7th row As 1st row.
8th row As 4th row.
These 8 rows form the rep of patt.

PANEL F

1st row [P4, K2] twice.
2nd row P2, K4, P2, C4B.
3rd row As 1st row.
4th row [P2, K4] twice.
5th row As 1st row.
6th row P2, C4B, P2, K4.
7th row As 1st row.
8th row As 4th row.
These 8 rows form the rep of patt.

BACK

With 5½ mm (No. 5/US 8) needles cast on 92(104: 116) sts.
1st row (RS) P2, [K4, P2] to end.
2nd row K2, [P4, K2] to end.
3rd and 4th rows As 1st and 2nd rows.
5th row P2, [C4B, P2] to end.
6th row As 2nd row.
Rep these 6 rows twice more.
Inc row [Patt 2, inc in next st] 8(10: 12) times, P2, [K4, P2] twice, [inc in next st, K1] 8 times, P2, [K4, P2] twice, [inc in next st, patt 2] 8(10: 12) times. 116(132: 148) sts.
Change to 6½ mm (No. 3/US 10) needles and cont in patt as folls:
1st row * [K1, P1, K1] into next st, P3 tog; rep from * 2(4: 6) times more **, work 12 sts as 1st row of Panel D, work 8 sts as 1st row of Panel B, work 12 sts as 1st row of Panel E, work 28 sts as 1st row of Panel A, work 12 sts as 1st row of Panel F, work 8 sts as 1st row of Panel B, work 12 sts as 1st row of Panel C; rep from * to ** once more.
2nd row P 12(20: 28), work 12 sts as 2nd row of Panel C, work 8 sts as 2nd row of Panel B, work 12 sts as 2nd row of Panel F, work 28 sts as 2nd row of Panel A, work 12 sts as 2nd row of Panel E, work 8 sts as 2nd row of Panel B, work 12 sts as 2nd row of Panel D, P to end.
3rd row * P3 tog, [K1, P1, K1] into next st; rep from * 2(4: 6) times more **, work 12 sts as 3rd row of Panel D, work 8 sts as 3rd row of Panel B, work 12 sts as 3rd row of Panel E, work 28 sts as 3rd row of Panel A, work 12 sts as 3rd row of Panel F, work 8 sts as 3rd row of Panel B, work 12 sts as 3rd row of Panel C; rep from * to ** once more.
4th row P 12(20: 28), work 12 sts as 4th row of Panel C, work 8 sts as 4th row of Panel B, work 12 sts as 4th row of Panel F, work 28 sts as 4th row of Panel A, work 12 sts as 4th row of Panel E, work 8 sts as 4th row of Panel B, work 12 sts as 4th row of Panel D, P to end.
These 4 rows form the rep of Trinity st at each end. Keeping Panel sts correct throughout and end sts as set, cont until work meas 66(70: 74) cm [26(27½: 29¼) ins] from beg, ending with a WS row.

Shape Shoulders

Keeping patt correct, cast off 11(14: 17) sts at beg of next 4 rows, then 12(14: 16) sts at beg of foll 2 rows.
Leave rem 48 sts on a holder for collar.

FRONT

Work as given for Back until front meas 58(62: 66) cm [22¾(24½: 26) ins] from beg, ending with a WS row.

Shape Neck

Next row Patt 44(52: 60), turn and leave rem sts on a spare needle.
Keeping patt correct, dec one st at neck edge on next 8 rows, then every foll alt row until 34(42: 50) sts rem.
Cont without shaping until work meas same as Back to shoulders, ending with a WS row.

Shape Shoulder

Keeping patt correct, cast off 11(14: 17) sts at beg of next and foll alt row.
Work 1 row straight, then cast off rem 12(14: 16) sts.
Return to sts on spare needle; with RS facing sl first 28 sts on to a holder for collar, rejoin yarn to neck edge and patt to end.
Cont to match first side, reversing all shaping.

SLEEVES

With 5½ mm (No. 5/US 8) needles cast on 36(42: 48) sts.
1st row (RS) [P1, K4, P1] to end.
2nd row [K1, P4, K1] to end.
3rd and 4th rows As 1st and 2nd rows.
5th row [P1, C4B, P1] to end.
6th row As 2nd row.
Rep these 6 rows twice more.
Inc row Patt 0(1: 3), [inc in next st, K1, inc in next st] to last 0(2: 3) sts, patt 0(2: 3). 60(68: 76) sts.
Change to 6½ mm (No. 3/US 10) needles and cont in patt as folls:
1st row * [K1, P1, K1] into next st, P3 tog; rep from * 0(1: 2) times more **, work 12 sts as 1st row of Panel E, work 28 sts as 1st row of Panel A, work 12 sts as 1st row of Panel F; rep from * to ** once more.
2nd row P 4(8: 12), work 12 sts as 2nd row of Panel F, work 28 sts as 2nd row

of Panel A, work 12 sts as 2nd row of Panel E, P to end.

This sets position of patt. Keeping Panel sts correct throughout and end sts in Trinity st, *at the same time*, inc one st at each end of the 3rd and every foll 4th row, until there are 92(100: 108) sts.

Cont without shaping until work meas 43(46: 48) cm [17(18: 19) ins] from beg, ending with a WS row.

Cast off *loosely*.

COLLAR

Join right shoulder seam.

With 5½ mm (No. 5/US 8) needles and RS facing, pick up and K 16 sts evenly down left front neck, K front neck sts from holder, pick up and K 16 sts evenly up right front neck, then K back neck sts from holder. 108 sts.

Beg with a 2nd row, work 14 cm (5½ ins) in rib as for Cuffs.

Cast off *loosely* in rib.

TO MAKE UP

Do not press.

Join left shoulder and collar seam. Sew in sleeves, with centre of sleeve to shoulder seam. Join side and sleeve seams. Fold collar in half to inside and sl st.

HIS AND HERS SADDLE SHOULDER SWEATER

MATERIALS

26(28) 50 g balls of Hayfield Brig Aran Classics.
1 pair each of 3¾ mm (No. 9/US 4) and 4½ mm (No. 7/US 6) knitting needles.
Set of four 3¾ mm (No. 9/US 4) double-pointed needles.
1 cable needle.

MEASUREMENTS

To fit Bust/ Chest	81–97 cm (102–117)	32–38 ins (40–46)
Length to shoulder	68 cm (72)	26¾ ins (28¼)
Sleeve seam	45 cm (48)	17¾ ins (19)

TENSION

20 sts and 25 rows to 10 cm (4 ins) over st st using 4½ mm (No. 7/US 6) needles.

ABBREVIATIONS

C4B–sl next 2 sts to cn to back of work, K2, then K2 from cn; C4F–sl next 2 sts to cn to front of work, K2, then K2 from cn; C6B–sl next 3 sts to cn to back of work, K3, then K3 from cn; C6F–sl next 3 sts to cn to front of work, K3, then K3 from cn; g st–garter stitch (every row K). Also see page 10.

PANEL A

1st row P2, K13, P2.
2nd row K2, P6, K1, P6, K2.
3rd row P2, K5, P1, K1, P1, K5, P2.
4th row K2, P4, [K1, P1] twice, K1, P4, K2.
5th row P2, K3, [P1, K1] 3 times, P1, K3, P2.
6th row K2, P2, [K1, P1] 4 times, K1, P2, K2.
7th row P2, K1, [P1, K1] 5 times, P1, K1, P2.
8th row As 6th row.
9th row As 5th row.
10th row As 4th row.
11th row As 3rd row.
12th row As 2nd row.
These 12 rows form the rep of patt.

PANEL B

1st row K4, P2, K12, P2, K4.
2nd row P4, K2, P12, K2, P4.
3rd row C4B, P2, C6B, C6F, P2, C4F.
4th row As 2nd row.
5th and 6th rows As 1st and 2nd rows.
7th row C4B, P2, K12, P2, C4F.
8th row As 2nd row.
9th and 10th rows As 1st and 2nd rows.
11th row As 3rd row.
12th row As 2nd row.
These 12 rows form the rep of patt.

BACK

With 3¾ mm (No. 9/US 4) needles cast on 98(118) sts.
1st row (RS) K2, [P2, K2] to end.
2nd row P2, [K2, P2] to end.
Rep these 2 rows until work meas 8 cm (3¼ ins) from beg, ending with a RS row.
Inc row Rib 1(3), m1, [rib 8(7), m1] 12(16) times, rib to end. 111(135) sts.
Change to 4½ mm (No. 7/US 6) needles and cont in patt as folls:
Beg with a K row, cont in st st until work meas 37 cm (14½ ins) from beg, ending with a P row.
Work 5 rows in g st.

Inc row K 7(12), [m1, K2, m1, K3] 20(23) times, K to end. 151(181) sts.

Next row P 2(0), [work 24(17) sts as 1st row of Panel B(A), work 17(24) sts as 1st row of Panel A(B)] 3(4) times, work 24(17) sts as 1st row of Panel B(A), P 2(0).

Next row K 2(0), [work 24(17) sts as 2nd row of Panel B(A), work 17(24) sts as 2nd row of Panel A(B)] 3(4) times, work 24(17) sts as 2nd row of Panel B(A), K 2(0).

This sets position of patt. Keeping Panel sts correct throughout and end sts on 1st size in reverse st st, cont until work meas approximately 64(68) cm [25¼(26¾) ins] from beg, ending with a 12th patt row.

Shape Shoulders

Cast off 48(60) sts at beg of next 2 rows.

Leave rem 55(61) sts on a holder for collar.

FRONT

Work as given for Back until front meas 60(64) cm [23½(25¼) ins] from beg, ending with a WS row.

Shape Neck

Next row Patt 63(76), turn and leave rem sts on a spare needle.

Keeping patt correct, cast off 4 sts at beg of next and foll 2 alt rows.

Dec one st at neck edge on next 3(4) rows. 48(60) sts.

Cont without shaping until work meas same as Back to shoulders, ending with same patt row.

Cast off.

Return to sts on spare needle; with RS facing sl first 25(29) sts on to a holder for collar, rejoin yarn to neck edge, cast off 4 sts and patt to end.

Cont to match first side, reversing shaping.

SLEEVES

With 3¾ mm (No. 9/US 4) needles cast on 42(46) sts and work 8 cm (3¼ ins) in rib as for Back welt, ending with a RS row.

Inc row Rib 4(1), m1, [rib 3(4), m1] 11 times, rib 5(1). 54(58) sts.

Change to 4½ mm (No. 7/US 6) needles and cont in patt as folls:

Beg with a K row cont in st st, inc one st at each end of the 5th and every foll 4th row until there are 74(78) sts.

Work 3 rows straight.

Work 5 rows in g st.

Inc row K 11(13), m1, [K4, m1] 13 times, K 11(13). 88(92) sts.

Next row K 15(17), work 17 sts as 1st row of Panel A, work 24 sts as 1st row of Panel B, work 17 sts as 1st row of Panel A, K 15(17).

Next row P 15(17), work 17 sts as 2nd row of Panel A, work 24 sts as 2nd row of Panel B, work 17 sts as 2nd row of Panel A, P 15(17).

This sets position of patt. Keeping Panel sts correct throughout and rem sts in st st, *at the same time*, inc one st at each end of next and every foll 4th row, until there are 110(118) sts.

Cont without shaping until work meas 45(48) cm [17¾(19) ins] from beg, ending with a WS row.

Shape Top

Keeping patt correct, cast off 41(45) sts at beg of next 2 rows. 28 sts.

Cont until work meas 63(70) cm [24¾(27½) ins] from beg, ending with a WS row.

Leave sts on a holder.

COLLAR

Sew row ends of sleeve tops to back and front shoulders.

With set of four 3¾ mm (No. 9/US 4) needles and RS facing, [K2 tog] 14 times across sts of left sleeve top, pick up and K 14(15) sts evenly down left front neck, K front neck sts from holder, dec 9 sts evenly across, then pick up and K 14(15) sts evenly up right front neck, [K2 tog] 14 times across sts of right sleeve top, then K back neck sts from holder dec 23 sts evenly across them. 104(116) sts.

Work 12 cm (4¾ ins) in rounds of K2, P2 rib.

Cast off *loosely* in rib.

TO MAKE UP

Do not press.

Sew in sleeves. Join side and sleeve seams.

Press seams lightly on WS according to instructions on ball band, omitting ribbing.